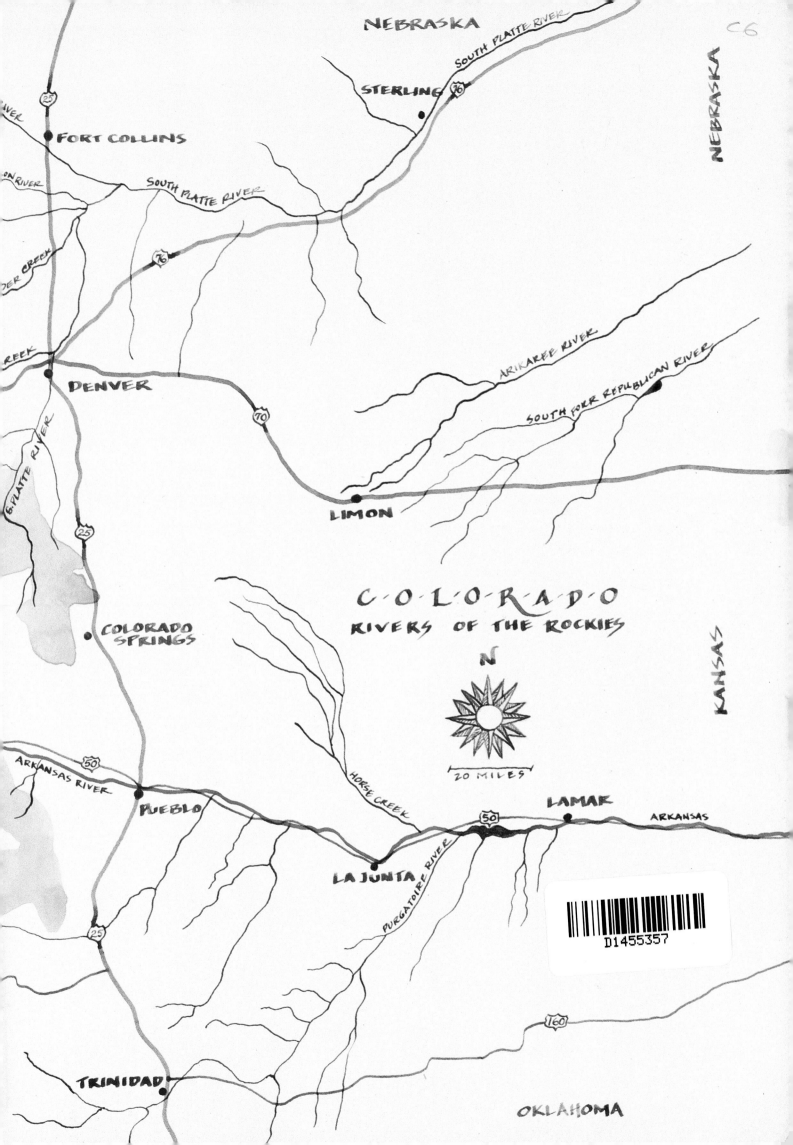

# COLORADO
# RIVERS OF THE ROCKIES

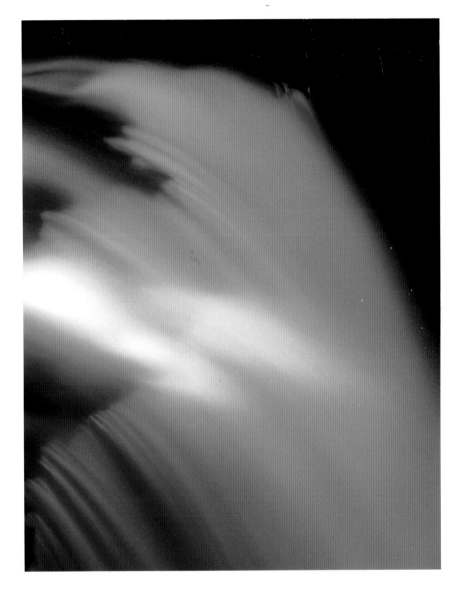

Photography by John Fielder
Text by Mark Pearson

Published in cooperation with
The Nature Conservancy of Colorado

WESTCLIFFE PUBLISHERS, INC.   ENGLEWOOD, COLORADO

# ACKNOWLEDGEMENTS

For the past five years I have been exploring, both on foot and by raft, Colorado's rivers. As with my llama-supported mountain travels, photographing in the wild with a large-format camera requires diligent help. On the river there is usually much more eating and drinking than on the typical mountain-photography excursion, consequently there is more food preparation and more empty beer cans to be hauled out.

I wish to thank the following for their help, support, and company on my travels: photographer Tom Till, a great artist as well as an accomplished boatman; my friend George Coale from Steamboat Springs; ski guide and river-wader Doug Lewis of Crested Butte; author Mark Pearson; and my family — my wife, Gigi, and our children, JT, Ashley, and Katy (all of whom have become useful and experienced river rats). In addition, I would like to thank Avon Seagull Marine for helping me acquire the best-made raft available.

Finally, I would like to dedicate this book to my family with the hope that it will motivate them to join me on future trips, thus allowing me to delegate such jobs as setting up the latrine and washing dishes each day!

— John Fielder

Wallace Stegner's "Overture" from *The Sound of Mountain Water* is reprinted with the permission of the author and Bantam, Doubleday, Dell Publishing.

A book as wide-ranging as one about Colorado's rivers necessarily draws on the talents and experience of many people. The late Steve Arrowsmith of Humpback Chub River Tours provided spiritual inspiration from many years of shared river adventures. Sydney Macy, Melinda Helmick, Alan Carpenter, Pat Willits, Robert Wigington, Mark Burget and the other staff members of The Nature Conservancy's Colorado office in Boulder extended invaluable insights and editorial suggestions. Dr. James Work of Colorado State University offered sage advice on early drafts, as did Dr. John Stednick. Publisher and photographer John Fielder was unwavering in his belief in my writing; editor Suzanne Venino and the rest of the staff at Westcliffe Publishers were equally supportive. And finally, thanks to my wife, Sherree Tatum, for her endless patience. — Mark Pearson

*Front Cover:* North Clear Creek Falls, a tributary of the Rio Grande, Rio Grande National Forest

*First Frontispiece:* Rabbitbrush along volcanic banks of the Rio Grande, San Luis Valley

*Second Frontispiece:* Rushing waters of Ruby Anthracite Creek flow through the Gunnison National Forest before reaching the Gunnison River

*Opposite:* Pillars of black schist, The Black Rocks of Ruby Canyon underlie sandstone along the Colorado River, Black Ridge Canyons BLM Wilderness Study Area

# CONTENTS

*Medano Creek at sunrise, Great Sand Dunes National Monument*
*Opposite: Grape Creek courses through the Wet Mountains before converging with the*
*Arkansas River, Lower Grape Creek BLM Wilderness Study Area*

# THE SOUND OF MOUNTAIN WATER

## FOREWORD

I discovered mountain rivers late, for I was a prairie child, and knew only flat-land and dryland until we toured the Yellowstone country in 1920, loaded with all the camp beds, auto tents, grub-boxes, and auxiliary water and gas cans that 1920 thought necessary. Our road between Great Falls, Montana, and Salt Lake City was the rutted track that is now Highway 89. Beside a marvelous torrent, one of the first I ever saw, we camped several days. That was Henry's Fork of the Snake.

I didn't know that it rose on the west side of Targhee Pass and flowed barely a hundred miles, through two Idaho counties, before joining the Snake near Rexburg; or that in 1810 Andrew Henry built on its bank near modern St. Anthony the first American post west of the continental divide. The divide itself meant nothing to me. My imagination was not stretched by the wonder of the parted waters, the Yellowstone rising only a few miles eastward to flow out toward the Missouri, the Mississippi, the Gulf, while this bright pounding stream was starting through its thousand miles of canyons to the Columbia and the Pacific.

All I knew was that it was pure delight to be where the land lifted in peaks and plunged in canyons, and to sniff air thin, spray-cooled, full of pine and spruce smells, and to be so close-seeming to the improbable indigo sky. I gave my heart to the mountains the minute I stood beside this river with its spray in my face and watched it thunder into foam, smooth to green glass over sunken rocks, shatter to foam again. I was fascinated by how it sped by and yet was always there; its roar shook both the earth and me.

When the sun dropped over the rim the shadows chilled sharply; evening lingered until foam on water was ghostly and luminous in the near-dark. Alders caught in the current sawed like things alive, and the noise was louder. It was rare and comforting to waken late and hear the undiminished shouting of the water in the night. And at sunup it was still there, powerful and incessant, with the slant sun tangled in its rainbow spray, the grass blue with wetness, and the air heady as ether and scented with campfire smoke.

By such a river it is impossible to believe that one will ever be tired or old. Every sense applauds it. Taste it, feel its chill on the teeth: it is purity absolute. Watch its racing current, its steady renewal of force: it is transient and eternal. And listen again to its sounds: get far enough away so that the noise of falling tons of water does not stun the ears, and hear how much is going on underneath a whole symphony of smaller sounds, hiss and splash and gurgle, the small talk of side channels, the whisper of blown and scattered spray gathering itself and beginning to flow again, secret and irresistible, among the wet rocks.

— WALLACE STEGNER

"Overture" from *The Sound Of Mountain Water* (1946)

---

*Big Dominguez Creek carves through rocks of black schist on its way to the Gunnison River, Dominguez Canyon BLM Wilderness Study Area*

# PREFACE

In *The Immense Journey*, Loren Eiseley writes that if there is magic on this planet, it is contained in water. It is that magic that has kept me under the spell of Colorado's rivers for as long as I can remember, drawing me to them again and again.

Memories surface of fishing with my father on the streams and creeks of South Park nearly 30 years ago. I can remember the waters teeming with trout, fed by an abundance of insects hatched among the dense willows that lined the banks of those verdant streams.

This scene dissolves into a recollection of a float trip down the Yampa River in 1984, a year of especially high water, and of being swallowed up by whitewater pandemonium only to be spit out into the river's gentle calm. It was in those tranquil moments that the river revealed itself and made me fully understand the need to protect the Yampa and the rest of Colorado's rivers.

That sense of urgency was driven home when I first saw the North Fork of the Cache la Poudre River from the rim of Phantom Canyon. Approaching the canyon, it was hard to imagine that a chasm even existed until I was standing on its precipice, overlooking a scene of such immense beauty that I knew it was no mere apparition. Phantom Canyon was acquired by The Nature Conservancy in 1987 and is now protected as one of the last roadless canyons along Colorado's Front Range.

It was because of the Conservancy's success at Phantom Canyon and on the Gunnison River, where we are working to establish precedent-setting water rights conversions, that we decided to launch the Rivers of the Rockies campaign. This ambitious effort will protect as much as 50,000 acres of streamside habitat and nearby grasslands on 21 Colorado rivers and their tributaries, areas that abound with mammals, birds, fish, insects, and plants. While riparian ecosystems occupy less than one percent of Colorado's total land area, they provide critical habitat for 60 percent of the state's wildlife.

To safeguard what little remains of these riparian areas, the Conservancy uses a cooperative, non-confrontational approach to find creative solutions to sensitive land and water issues. The Nature Conservancy is the foremost land conservation organization in the world, preserving biodiversity by protecting more than 6.5 million acres of valuable habitat over the past 40 years. Established nearly 30 years ago, the Conservancy's Colorado Program has since protected 70,000 acres throughout the state.

Since launching the Rivers of the Rockies campaign in 1988, we have had successes on the Piedra, Conejos, North St. Vrain, Rio Grande, Lake Fork of the Gunnison, and Purgatoire rivers. We are also working to protect lands along the Arikaree River, as well as a 13.5-mile stretch of the Animas.

On the San Miguel, one of the last free-flowing rivers in the western United States, the Conservancy has acquired three preserves, encompassing six river miles of some of the highest-quality riparian forest in Colorado. These preserves form the foundation of a long-term effort to safeguard most of the river and its major tributaries. Negotiations now under way with private landowners and public agencies will result in the protection of 40 additional miles.

The Conservancy recently set its sights on the Yampa River, where we are working to integrate human use of land and water resources with the preservation of biodiversity. Here the Conservancy is taking an ecosystem approach rather than focusing on specific preserves. As a result, migratory birds, native fishes, and riparian forests will be protected along with the ecosystems that sustain them. The Conservancy is also pursuing a strategy on the Yampa that we pioneered on the Gunnison — the acquisition of water rights. This acquisition will protect up to three-quarters of the annual water flow in the Yampa and eliminate the threat of two major dams.

While we have had many triumphs in our Rivers of the Rockies campaign, there are still many challenges ahead. The Conservancy is only one player in these conservation efforts; individuals like John Fielder also have a critical role. Through projects like this book and his work with the Conservancy, John uses his tremendous talent to raise awareness and underscore the need for action. It is through such efforts that the rivers of Colorado will be protected, and with them the astounding variety of life that has adapted to these ever-changing ecosystems.

— SYDNEY SHAFROTH MACY
Colorado Director
The Nature Conservancy

*The Yampa River as it passes beneath the Grand Overhang,
Dinosaur National Monument*

# INTRODUCTION

Colorado is naturally blessed with some of the most beautiful mountains in the world. I have spent much of the past twenty years exploring this alpine domain, and until five years ago I was content to only infrequently visit the rest of Colorado. But in 1987, on a rafting trip down the Green River in Dinosaur National Monument, I discovered a grand new landscape and its accompanying sights, sounds, smells, and, of course — photographs.

I think many people forget, or are simply not aware of, how many major river systems originate in Colorado. The Colorado River and its tributaries (the Dolores, the San Juan, and the Green, which originates in Wyoming) as well as the Green's tributaries (the Yampa and the White, which do begin in Colorado) drain the entire western slope of the Colorado Rockies. The North Platte courses northward toward its rendezvous with the South Platte, which drains the eastern slope of the Front Range.

Further south, snowmelt from the Sawatch and Sangre de Cristo ranges contributes most of the water in the Arkansas River as it flows eastward into Kansas (though agricultural demands sometime use all the river water before it gets there). Finally, the Rio Grande drains the eastern San Juan Mountains before the river enters New Mexico.

For more than a hundred years, these rivers and their mountain creeks have been the lifeblood of Colorado industry. Agriculture, the third largest industry in the state, and mining, at one time the mainstay of Colorado's economy, have always been the greatest consumers of water. Today, however, tourism — Colorado's second largest and fastest growing industry — is more dependent than ever upon the amount of water flowing in these rivers. Why? Because recreational use of our rivers is increasing rapidly.

From Pumphouse to State Bridge on the Colorado, through Brown's Canyon on the Arkansas, upside down through Snaggletooth Rapid on the Dolores and sideways through the Yampa's Warm Springs Rapid in Dinosaur National Monument...several hundred thousand people a year enjoy whitewater boating on Colorado rivers. In addition, fishing adds $600 million to the state's economy each year.

As Colorado evolves from a dependency upon "extractive" industry to a reliance upon "attractive" industry, its citizens must consider new water priorities. Water for recreation means that our rivers must flow freely, without the impediment of dams. We must there-fore think twice before building new ones. In addition, Coloradans need to consider whether unused water stored in existing reservoirs should be released for the benefit of recreation, or merely held for agricultural uses in anticipation of drought years.

Even more important is the ecology of Colorado's river corridors. Too little water means that native fish as well as other fauna and flora cannot exist as nature intended. To correct deficiencies in water flow levels, and to protect habitat in riparian zones, The Nature Conservancy of Colorado has engaged itself ambitiously for years to come. Their efforts to seek donations from individuals, businesses, and foundations to protect both land and water have been enormously successful, yet much more remains to be done.

Westcliffe Publishers and I are pleased to be able to produce this book in cooperation with The Nature Conservancy. Through the writings of naturalist Mark Pearson, we hope this book will educate Coloradans about the challenges that face our rivers. I hope that this book will also stimulate a new awareness, through photographs of my own river travels during the past five years, of those parts of Colorado often overlooked in favor of our mountains.

Protecting our remaining wild places means not only preserving land in its natural condition, but investing time and money to insure that water flows freely and gener-ously in our creeks and rivers. We Coloradans must reconsider our priorities by seeking ways to both protect the natural environment and generate the greatest return on our investment. In the years ahead, you will read more and more about water use in Colorado and throughout the West. I urge you to listen carefully and to make your feelings about these matters known to your representa-tives in both state and federal legislatures.

And I hope that you, too, through the pages of this book, but preferably out of doors, will have the opportu-nity to enjoy the sights, sounds, and smells unique to Colorado's river places.

— JOHN FIELDER
Englewood, Colorado

*Rapids along the Green River, Dinosaur National Monument*

# THE SOUTH PLATTE

## DIVERSE APPROACHES TO PRESERVATION

The South Platte's watershed is the largest of any river in Colorado, which is fitting since the majority of Colorado's population resides in its drainage. As the river traverses its basin from the Continental Divide to the Nebraska border, it spans life zones as diverse as alpine tundra and prairie grasslands. At its source, high in the snowcapped peaks of the Mosquito Range, the river consists of little more than cascading rivulets and murmuring brooks. Out on the prairie, the historic South Platte was once described in spring flood stage as a mile wide and an inch deep.

As befits the South Platte's diversity, river proponents have employed a number of approaches to preserve its natural attributes. Where environmental factors combine to create ecosystems rich in biological diversity, private and public organizations have purchased these lands to remove the threat of development. Where significant stretches of the river remained free flowing, citizens resorted to federal legislation that prohibits dams and inappropriate riverside development. And where major dams threatened to disrupt river ecology over large areas, alternatives were promoted for meeting the water needs of metropolitan regions.

One particularly diverse ecosystem lies near the headwaters of the South Platte. Some 8,000 years ago, Ice Age glaciers retreated from what is today High Creek Fen, a 900-acre wetland in South Park. A fen is distinguished from more common wetlands by the presence of peat, or partially decomposed plant material, which has accumulated since the last glacial age. Biologists with The Nature Conservancy have rated High Creek Fen as the most ecologically diverse fen in the southern Rocky Mountains. It is home to at least ten state-rare plant species, nearly all of which are what botanists call arctic, or boreal, disjuncts, meaning these species are locally rare populations more commonly found in Alaska and the northern Rockies.

As any home gardener knows, peat is valued as a soil conditioner, and this commercial value threatened High Creek Fen. After 20 acres were strip-mined for peat, the Conservancy moved to preempt additional destruction of the fen, and in 1991 the Conservancy raised $700,000 to buy and maintain it. Through its prompt action, the Conservancy ensured that the fen's many rare plants will not be harmed by future development.

Another example of biological richness is found on a tributary of the South Platte along Colorado's densely populated northern Front Range. There, on the North Fork of the Cache la Poudre River, a wild canyon has eluded Colorado's widening circle of urbanization. Along one of the last roadless canyons in the Front Range, this unspoiled valley, called Phantom Canyon by locals, offers sanctuary to many large and shy predators, provides refuge for raptors such as golden and bald eagles, and supports a highly productive trout fishery. And as is often the case, this secluded canyon harbors a number of rare plants. The largest known population of *Aletes humilis*, a globally rare parsley, grows in Phantom Canyon.

Clearly, such a wild gem was unlikely to remain undamaged in the face of growing Front Range demand for 40-acre mountain subdivision sites. The Conservancy stepped forward and purchased 1,120 acres outright while negotiating with adjacent landowners for protective easement on another 480 acres. All told, six miles of river were protected and today Phantom Canyon is managed by the Conservancy.

Where significant stretches of a river remain free flowing, one tool for preservation is the federal Wild and Scenic Rivers Act. When a river is listed under this act, additional dams and water development are precluded along the designated reach. Land-use restrictions are also placed on adjacent riverbank property up to a quarter mile on either side of the river. Many Colorado rivers have been studied for inclusion in the system, but the only river so designated is the Cache la Poudre River, the South Platte's largest tributary.

The Cache la Poudre saw much of the earliest water development in Colorado. Pioneers harnessed the river's spring snowmelt through a series of high mountain reservoirs on its tributaries. Trans-basin diversions were constructed to transport water from the Colorado, North Platte, and Laramie rivers and channel it to Colorado's eastern plains to irrigate crops. All this was accomplished without any main-stem reservoirs, however, so by the 1970s the Poudre's canyon still retained its wild nature. Nonetheless, a half-dozen reservoirs existed in various stages of planning, several of which would flood extensive reaches of river. Northern Colorado citizens encouraged Congress to authorize a wild and scenic study for the river. When the U.S. Forest Service recommended wild and scenic designation for long stretches of the Poudre, citizens followed up with additional pressure for congressional action. Finally, in 1986, after several years of intensive negotiations between the water development

---

*Sunset in Phantom Canyon, a Nature Conservancy preserve along the North Fork of the Cache la Poudre River, a tributary of the South Platte*

community, environmental organizations, and local landowners, Congress enacted legislation adding more than 70 miles of the Poudre to the National Wild and Scenic Rivers System.

To be included in the system, a river must possess values that the law vaguely defines as "outstandingly remarkable." Finding such outstandingly remarkable values is not difficult on a river as noteworthy as the Poudre. The Poudre begins at Milner Pass in Rocky Mountain National Park and flows through park land and the adjacent Comanche Peak Wilderness Area for 17 miles. Called the Big South at this point, the river meanders through wide subalpine meadows and cuts a short but deep gorge before it parallels Highway 14 through Poudre Canyon. From there, the river's ready accessibility lures anglers and campers by the score, and any summer day will find dozens of rafters and kayakers running its rapids.

Back on the South Platte main stem, the South Platte Canyon supports a celebrated trout fishery just 30 miles north of Denver. First actively promoted by tourist-seeking railroads in the 1880s, the river is still known for its sizable rainbow and brown trout, and it is rated by wildlife managers as a Gold Medal fishery. The occurrence of such remarkable fishing just outside the Rocky Mountain West's largest metropolitan area is most unusual, and the combination of sparkling waters and crisp mountain air conspires to attract more than just anglers. The river's ready accessibility to Denver draws many others interested in camping, inner-tubing, or just picnicking along the lazy river.

Given the South Platte Canyon's popularity, the furor caused by the Denver Water Department's proposed Two Forks Dam at the confluence of the river's North and South forks came as little surprise. Rather than lose the recreational amenities provided by the South Platte Canyon, and fearing far-ranging ecological impacts to migratory birds downstream in Nebraska, environmental groups developed a positive vision for meeting Denver's water needs without another large main-stem dam on the South Platte. These groups recruited scientists and engineers who employed the same technical tools used by dam builders. In 1982, the Environmental Caucus unveiled its first substantial technical alternative to Two Forks. The alternative relied on a variety of small-scale approaches to developing additional water supplies. Among the ideas were increased emphasis on water conservation,

including metering the 80,000 Denver homes still without water meters; construction of smaller reservoirs or enlargement of existing ones; and innovative water management programs such as leasing water from downstream farmers, using the water, and then returning treated wastewater to the farmers for irrigation.

This approach by river proponents ultimately proved successful. Moved by the apparent environmental inadequacies of the Two Forks Dam and the availability of alternatives, the U.S. Environmental Protection Agency vetoed issuance of a critical federal permit. In response to the veto, managers at the Denver Water Department developed a new agenda that emphasized water conservation, construction of smaller projects, and innovative water management policies — many of the same approaches advocated by environmental groups. In the aftermath of Two Forks, the water department completed installation of water meters by 1992, eight years ahead of schedule and $3 million under budget.

Many more approaches exist for safeguarding rivers and their natural ecosystems. On rivers constrained by dams, for example, the challenge lies in finding enough water to sustain ecological processes downstream. In one such case on the Gunnison River, The Nature Conservancy is working to secure precedent-setting water rights by converting reservoir rights to streamflow rights. On rivers less modified by water diversion and storage, such as the Yampa, the task is to preserve the large-scale ecological processes that have shaped the river itself, as well as its aquatic life and riparian plant communities. There, the Conservancy is working to implement a bioreserve program that incorporates the preservation of native ecosystems with current and future human demands. All told, the approaches to river preservation are as varied as there are rivers in Colorado. The challenge is finding the right approach for each river and then moving quickly.

---

*West Branch of the Laramie River descends to the North Platte River, Rawah Wilderness*
*Overleaf: Sunset on the South Platte River, near Fort Morgan*

Four large intermontane valleys, or parks, form a line across Colorado's middle from Wyoming to New Mexico. The northernmost of these is, not surprisingly, called North Park. North, Middle, and South parks were left behind as faulting and folding warped surrounding mountain ranges skyward. Rivers exiting these parks carved precipitous canyons to breach the encircling mountains. In the case of North Park, the North Platte River cuts Northgate Canyon through the Medicine Bow Mountains into southern Wyoming. Because of their location amidst less hospitable high country, the parks served as winter refuges for big game herds. Native Americans called North Park the "bull pen," in reference to its large herds of bison. While bison no longer roam North Park, it still serves as winter range for large numbers of elk, mule deer, and pronghorn.

*Sunrise on the North Platte River, North Park*

More than 400 kettle ponds, many covered with dense, floating mats of vegetation, provide one of Colorado's more uncommon features near Big Creek Lakes on the western fringe of North Park. Formed 8,000 years ago when blocks of buried glacial ice melted, these ponds are now home to a diverse array of rare and threatened Colorado plants and amphibians. The wood frog, a Colorado threatened species, is one of three frog species that makes this area home. Even more unusual is the presence of the roundleaf sundew, a carnivorous plant known to exist in only one other location in Colorado. The sundew typically grows in nitrogen-poor environments and supplements its nitrogen intake with hapless insects caught on sticky hairs that cover the plant's leaves. The Nature Conservancy has proposed that this unusual habitat be designated an official Research Natural Area by Routt National Forest, which manages the land.

*Lily pads blanket a kettle pond near the headwaters of the North Fork of the North Platte River,*
*Routt National Forest*

Twelve moose, fresh from Utah's Uinta Mountains, were released at Big Bottom on the Illinois River in 1978. Along with several dozen other moose that were later released in North Park and across the Rawah Range along the Laramie River, these animals formed the pioneer stock for a herd that now numbers between 500 and 600. The Colorado Division of Wildlife reintroduced moose here in the belief that the animals were original inhabitants eradicated by excessive hunting early in Colorado's history. Division wildlife biologists also determined that moose would occupy a void in this habitat because, unlike deer and elk which migrate in winter from the surrounding forests down onto the open range of North Park, moose would stay in the coniferous forest on the fringes of the park year-round.

*The Illinois River meanders through North Park before joining the North Platte River*

*Headwaters of the South Platte River, Mosquito Creek drains the slopes of the Mosquito Range,
Pike National Forest, with Pikes Peak in the distance*

*The South Platte River cascades through Waterton Canyon near Denver,
its final mountain run before entering the Great Plains*

Waterton Canyon marks the northern terminus of the 470-mile Colorado Trail, which connects Denver with Durango via a circuitous route through mountains and valleys. Officially dedicated in 1988, after more than ten years of work by 3,000 volunteers representing every state in the union, the Colorado Trail links many of the state's river valleys. The trail begins along the South Platte southwest of Denver and crosses over to the Arkansas River, skirting the Collegiate Range. It then traverses the headwaters of the Gunnison River and the Rio Grande before dropping into the Animas drainage for the homestretch to Durango. Hiking the trail gives one an unforgettable sense of Colorado's watershed topography. To hike the entire length of the trail at once takes six to seven weeks, although many hikers complete it in shorter segments.

*Winter waters of the West Fork of Clear Creek feed the South Platte River,*
*Arapaho National Forest*

Although one-third of Colorado consists of high plains and shortgrass prairie, this province is largely forgotten when it comes to rivers. When the U.S. Department of the Interior inventoried Colorado's outstanding rivers in 1981, distinctive landscapes were discovered along 48 miles of the Arikaree and 150 miles of the Purgatoire. Rivers of the eastern plains are usually best remembered for their historical significance, such as the 1868 battle between Cheyenne Indians and the U.S. Cavalry at the Arikaree's Beecher Island. But when one visits these high, lonesome prairie rivers today, the landscape evokes primeval images. Pausing along their banks, one almost expects to see a herd of bison come thundering into view, perhaps chased by aboriginal hunters, like a scene straight out of the movie *Dances with Wolves*.

*Summer thunderstorms swell a normally dry streambed of the Arikaree River, a tributary of the Republican River, which eventually flows into the Missouri River*

*Spring along the North Saint Vrain River, a tributary of the South Platte River and part of The Nature Conservancy's North Saint Vrain Creek Preserve*

# THE ARKANSAS

## MEETING COMPETING DEMANDS

High in the Sawatch Range, at the rooftop of the Rockies, the tundra reaches saturation in late spring as melting snow infiltrates the thin soil. Pools collect in shallow depressions and rivulets twist and wind through clumps of tundra grasses. A tiny water droplet sparkles in the brilliant alpine sunshine and pauses ever so precariously at the lip of a melting snowbank before gravity finally tugs it loose and sends it on its way. But to where?

This droplet, like so many others, takes form on the eastern flank of Mt. Massive. Gravity and geography dictate that it run to the Arkansas River. Along its route, rafters will likely float buoyed by it, anglers will pursue trout through whose gills it has passed, farmers may spread it among cantaloupes near Rocky Ford, and, if it hasn't yet evaporated, the droplet may find its way 1,000 miles down the Arkansas to the mighty Mississippi. Along the way the droplet also unfortunately encounters countless molecules of sulfuric acid, and compounds containing zinc, cadmium, and many other elements released during decades of hardrock mining. These effluents can diminish the water's usefulness to both ecological systems and human endeavors.

The growing recreational use of rivers runs headlong into the remnants of historic mining in few places as it does on the upper Arkansas River. In 1992, more than a half-million recreational users visited the Arkansas headwaters, and nearly 200,000 people rafted the river. Its nationally renowned whitewater rapids prove a potent attraction when combined with close proximity to Denver and other Front Range metropolitan centers. And anglers demand a productive trout fishery from a river fed by Colorado's highest peaks.

Bowing to the inevitable, local, state, and federal governments joined hands in 1989 to create a partnership aimed at enhancing recreation opportunities along the Arkansas. A cooperative management agreement was signed between the federal Bureau of Land Management (BLM), which administers 60,000 acres of public land along the river, and the Colorado Division of Parks and Outdoor Recreation. Under the agreement, the division of parks made major facility improvements, such as campgrounds and boat ramps, and the BLM increased its interpretative efforts. Even local towns and counties participated in this partnership. Both Salida and Buena Vista used state lottery funds and federal conservation dollars to construct riverfront parks that tied in with the network of state and federal facilities.

The deluge of anglers and whitewater boaters has cast sleepy communities like Salida and Buena Vista into the forefront of Colorado's booming recreational market. This shift in local economy offers a solid indicator of changing water-use priorities. Tourism generated by the Arkansas River represents the number one source of revenue in Chaffee County, and the Colorado Tourism Board estimates that the three upper Arkansas Valley counties ring up $25 to $30 million annually from recreation.

Some might argue that the boom in recreation is but one more in a long line of exploitive uses of the river. Commercial rafting quadrupled between 1982 and 1992, and hordes of people usually bring concomitant resource impacts such as litter, stream-bank erosion, and crowding. At the height of the rafting season, as many as 450 boats per day pass through Brown's Canyon, a popular whitewater stretch. Divided into a typical seven- or eight-hour day, this amounts to one raft every minute.

Surging recreational demand, and the resultant state and federal partnership necessary to deal with it, led to resource management that actually reduced environmental damage to levels below those of 10 years ago, according to Pete Zwaneveld, the BLM's Arkansas River manager. "Hardening parking areas and boat ramps reduced erosion and concentrated impact in localized areas, improving the environment," Zwaneveld explains. Commercial outfitters were restricted as to where they could stop and picnic and were also required to use porta-potties to haul out human waste. Zwaneveld believes that outfitters police themselves well. Each year he patrols the river to assess environmental impact and is pleasantly surprised by the lack of such problems as trash, human waste, and trees damaged by firewood gatherers.

The Arkansas's recreational users exemplify the changing attitudes toward appropriate use of Colorado's water resources. For one thing, whitewater rafters require sufficient streamflow to negotiate rapids. And secondly, anglers (and to a lesser extent rafters) need water above a basic minimum standard of quality to pursue their sport. Despite the challenge in accommodating yet another player in a tightly regulated water-supply system, as well as the effort and expense of cleaning up pollution left behind by 19th century mining, these new recreational users are demanding restoration of what is an increasingly scarce resource — natural, free-flowing rivers.

Water supply poses a major challenge for the upper Arkansas. The Bureau of (Continued on page 32)

---

*Stained red by the runoff from mine tailings, the tainted water of South Fork of Lake Creek flows to the Arkansas River, San Isabel National Forest*
*Overleaf: The Purgatoire River, as seen from The Nature Conservancy's OV Mesa*

Reclamation's Twin Lakes Reservoir sits astride Lake Creek, and the pattern of water releases from the reservoir largely determines the flow of the Arkansas in late summer. The Bureau, along with most water users, traditionally viewed the river as nothing more than a conduit to transport water diverted from the Fryingpan and Eagle rivers to downstream cities and farms. But in 1992, as water manager for the entire river, the Bureau participated in a water-flow study designed to determine if recreational use could peacefully coexist with established agricultural and municipal uses. In response to public interest in extending the rafting season, the Bureau experimented with a modified schedule of water releases that provided higher streamflows in late summer.

Additional late summer water releases did not please all recreational users, however. Trout fishermen hoping to turn the Arkansas into another of Colorado's famed Gold Medal fisheries feared the higher flows would disrupt brown trout spawning by stressing the trout at a time the fish should be gaining strength. The disagreement between anglers and rafters grew rancorous at times. The argument's vehemence was curious in that fishermen and rafters argued more about the proper allocation of water among their competing recreational interests than they did about traditional water uses such as irrigation and municipal consumption.

Water quality is the other major challenge facing the Arkansas. At the turn of the century, several large drainage tunnels were constructed in the Arkansas's headwaters to divert unwanted water from dozens of mines. Not surprisingly, this highly acidic water, which contained elevated levels of dissolved metals, devastated aquatic life for many miles downstream. Industrial pollution, whether caused by mining or other activities, was recognized as a widespread national problem by the early 1980s. In response to citizen pressure, Congress enacted legislation to clean up heavily polluted abandoned sites. Commonly known as the Superfund law, the legislation required that, wherever possible, those responsible for pollution pay for its remediation. Several of the most severely polluted sites in Colorado included on the Superfund cleanup list were mine drainage tunnels, two of them in the Arkansas watershed.

California Gulch, downstream from the effluent of the Yak Tunnel, has been called the most polluted watershed in the Arkansas drainage. The U.S. Environmental Protection Agency blames high levels of copper, zinc, lead, and cadmium from mines in California Gulch for elevated toxicity levels in the Arkansas as far downstream as Salida, some 70 miles of river.

Another major tunnel is the Leadville Drain, located in the East Fork drainage and acquired by the Bureau of Reclamation after World War II as a means of consolidating water rights. Unfortunately for the Bureau, it acquired responsibility for the pollution along with the water rights, and the chronic metal toxicity contributed by the Leadville Drain was blamed for drastically reducing the numbers and size of trout in the Arkansas main stem. In this instance, the Bureau's mandate for developing agricultural water supplies created a new imperative, that of restoring streams to a fishable and swimmable state. As a consequence, the Bureau, using public tax dollars, constructed a wastewater treatment plant for the Leadville Drain in 1992.

Perhaps it is ironic that fishermen battle rafters about flow levels in a river plagued with chronic metal toxicity. Heavy-metal pollution does not adversely affect trout reproduction; it instead reduces longevity, and consequently it is uncommon to find trout more than three years old in the Arkansas. If the new water treatment plants on headwater tributaries take a noticeable bite out of heavy-metal pollution, trout life span and size should increase noticeably.

For the foreseeable future, recreation is here to stay as a preferred use of the Arkansas River. Coloradans today place a high value on the recreational uses of free-flowing rivers, and this shift in public attitude has dictated the redirection of priorities and policies among state and federal agencies. Active remediation of past mining pollution continues in the Arkansas headwaters, and water managers have modified the river's flow to reflect new recreational demands. As is so often the case in a democracy, the citizenry leads and the government follows. For the Arkansas River, the result is biological rebirth and newfound appreciation for recreational opportunities.

*Chalk Creek drains Mount Princeton and part of the majestic Sawatch Range, San Isabel National Forest*

Railroads afforded the major means of transportation across Colorado in the late 1800s. Dozens of railroad companies and lines sprang forth — often in bloodthirsty competition with each other — to service booming mines and their attendant industries. One of the many branches of the Denver & Rio Grande ran along Grape Creek from Canon City to Westcliffe, hauling silver and iron ore out of the Wet Mountain valley. This narrow-gauge line crossed Grape Creek 35 times and, not surprisingly, was most susceptible to floods. Constructed in 1881, the line was immediately washed out, then rebuilt in 1884. A greater flood in 1889 again obliterated much of the line, and as a result it was abandoned. Today, hikers can follow the old grade and still find occasional rails embedded in the stream bottom or on the hillside. After looking at the tight, sheer canyon walls, visitors can only marvel at the optimism of early railroad engineers.

*Enjoyed by more than 100,000 rafters each year, the Arkansas River courses through pastoral farmland near Nathrop*

*A narrow-gauge railroad once paralleled Grape Creek, though little evidence remains today,*
*Lower Grape Creek BLM Wilderness Study Area*

The Rocky Mountains reach their highest point in central Colorado. Here, fifteen peaks of the Sawatch and Collegiate ranges extend higher than 14,000 feet above sea level, including 14,421-foot Mount Massive, Colorado's second-highest peak. Winter snowstorms build deep drifts among these rocky promontories, which demarcate the spine of the Continental Divide. Throughout the spring and summer, melting snow supplies the vast majority of streamflows in Colorado. Mighty rivers, like the Arkansas, take form as puddles and rivulets high in the alpine tundra. These trickles combine and grow as they drop thousands of feet to the valleys below, until finally enough converge to gain status as an official river.

*Evening light at Notch Lake, headwaters of Busk Creek and the Arkansas River,*
*Mount Massive Wilderness*

Southern Colorado's Sangre de Cristo Mountains are the state's only fault-block range. The Sangres were thrust skyward approximately 28 million years ago. Geologists hypothesize that as this region of Colorado warped upward, large faults developed on either side of the San Luis Valley, and the entire valley stayed put while mountains rose around it. The steep, jagged western face of the Sangres marks one large fault zone. Today, the Sangres are one of Colorado's most abrupt ranges, soaring 7,000 vertical feet in a horizontal distance of just two to three miles. The exaggerated elevational gradient creates innumerable cascades and waterfalls as melting snow coalesces into rushing mountain streams and plunges toward the surrounding San Luis and Wet Mountain valleys.

*North Colony Creek plunges down cliffs in the Sangre de Cristo Mountains, San Isabel National Forest*

Scientists have zeroed in on remote and pristine alpine lakes in Colorado's high country in their search for better information about the prevalence of acid precipitation. Pollutants like sulfur dioxide and nitrous oxides generated by automobiles and power plants find their way into transcontinental air masses. While in the atmosphere, these pollutants change into sulfuric and nitric acids and then fall to earth in the form of rain or snow. Wilderness lakes in the Colorado Rockies offer an ideal natural laboratory for scientists to estimate the abundance and impact of acid precipitation. The U.S. Environmental Protection Agency directs an ongoing monitoring and research program that measures acid precipitation in many areas throughout Colorado and elsewhere in the West.

*Headwaters of North Halfmoon Creek, elevation of 13,000 feet, Mount Massive Wilderness*

*North Halfmoon Creek descends from peaks of the Sawatch Range, Mount Massive Wilderness*
*Overleaf: Evening thundershowers in the Sangre de Cristo Mountains will eventually*
*drain into the Arkansas River*

# THE RIO GRANDE

## WETLANDS AND WATERFOWL

Thirty million years ago, the North American midriff bulged from the collision of continents. To the west, the uplift pushed the Colorado Plateau skyward. To the east, a chain of mountains, the Rockies, reached higher and higher. Tectonic forces thrust and twisted granitic bedrock into towering ranges. Giant fissures opened to the surface from underground magma caverns, spewing rivers of molten rock that poured over the rising ranges of the San Juan Mountains in southwestern Colorado.

As the land warped upward, the unrelenting strain of tectonic forces stretched and swelled it beyond its limits. Along the present-day course of the Rio Grande, linear fault systems hundreds of miles long relieved the pressure, and a massive expanse of continental rock slipped downward as surrounding ranges were uplifted. The entire Rio Grande Valley appeared to settle deeper and deeper as the warping continued. All the while, water and wind scoured the newly formed mountains, and sediments poured into the giant rift valley left between the ranges. By the time the orogeny, or mountain building, ceased, the floor of the rift zone's upper end lay buried beneath more than 10,000 feet of sediments and volcanic ash in the San Luis Valley, bounded by the upthrust fault block of the Sangre de Cristo Mountains and the fuming volcanic massif of the San Juan Range.

Geology and topography combined to create the conflicting landscapes seen in the San Luis Valley today — a high, dry desert covered by alkaline marshes and wetlands. The San Juans and Sangre de Cristos catch moisture-laden winter storms and accumulate deep snowpacks. Melting snow feeds innumerable mountain streams that rush headlong down the mountains' flanks. The streams eventually stall in the shifting sands of the northern valley and sink into unconsolidated sediments. Shallow, impermeable layers of clay trap the water near the surface, creating a high groundwater table. Surface expressions of this groundwater form the ubiquitous wetlands and lakes of the San Luis Valley.

The San Juan and Sangre de Cristo mountains, which ring the valley like pincers, left a constricted opening at the valley's southern end. This narrow neck funnels migrating birds and waterfowl between the ranges, creating a sub-migrational flyway from the Gulf of Mexico to the mountains of southern Colorado. The San Luis Valley's pervasive wetlands, situated in an otherwise desert environment, attract vast flocks of migratory waterfowl. Numerous species of ducks nest here: cinnamon teal, blue-winged teal, mallards, pintails, and redheads. Many other notable species grace the shores: snowy plovers (now a candidate for endangered species protection), white-faced ibis, Canada geese, and — a favorite of bird watchers — sandhill cranes.

Upwards of 20,000 sandhill cranes pause here for six to eight weeks on their migration from wintering grounds in New Mexico's Bosque del Apache refuge to summer breeding areas at Gray's Lake in Idaho. Few would argue with the crane's impressive appearance — standing four feet tall with wingspans as great as seven feet. Accompanying the majestic sandhills are a handful of endangered whooping cranes. In an attempt to supplement the primary flock of whooping cranes that winters along the Gulf of Mexico, wildlife managers transplanted baby whoopers into the Gray's Lake sandhill flock, hoping the whoopers would mate with each other as adults, thus establishing a secondary flock. Successful breeding has not occurred, however, so while the whoopers delight visitors, the ecological experiment has yet to succeed.

Over the years, humans extensively altered the valley's wetlands in their quest for arable cropland. Some wetlands were drained and others channelized, severely disrupting the natural aquatic cycle of the ecosystem. As compensation for this habitat destruction, two federal wildlife refuges were established along the Rio Grande — the Alamosa and Monte Vista national wildlife refuges. Elsewhere in the valley, state and federal game managers, in conjunction with the Bureau of Reclamation's Closed Basin water development project, flooded naturally shallow lakes, such as San Luis Lake, in an effort to further mitigate lost waterfowl habitat.

These actions slowed the decline in waterfowl populations, and the valley is still the most productive waterfowl breeding habitat in Colorado. In fact, it comprises the southernmost waterfowl breeding area in the central flyway. But this apparent success highlights the pitfalls of single-species game management. Namely, when managers focus on only one component of the ecosystem, they lose sight of the fundamental ecological dictum that all parts are interconnected, even if in ways little understood. In this instance, inundating the naturally shallow saline lakes benefitted waterfowl, but it also increased pressure on certain native plant species.

One such plant that has felt the impact of water management policies is *Cleome multicaulis,* an inconspicuous annual also known as the many-stemmed spider-flower,

---

*Middle Fork of the Conejos River plummets over a volcanic escarpment, South San Juan Wilderness*

or little beeplant. *Cleome* grows in the saline environs of the San Luis Valley characterized by greasewood and saltbush communities. Because these lakes are surface expressions of the groundwater, some scientists theorize that the lakes respond to cycles of groundwater increase and decrease resulting from variations in runoff from the surrounding snowpack. As the lakes recede, *Cleome* advances; as the lakes grow, *Cleome* retreats to higher ground. *Cleome* thus evolved in an environment that depended on the slow-paced hydro cycles of the lakes. Managers interested in maintaining constant, deeper lake levels for both waterfowl and recreation have placed the survival of *Cleome* in question.

As with so many plants, relatively little is known about the extent and requirements of *Cleome*. It exists in widely separate, disjunct populations in Colorado, New Mexico, and elsewhere in the Southwest, perhaps spread between these divergent sites by the action of birds. Although populations of *Cleome* have been identified at other shallow lakes in the San Luis Valley, it has been proposed for designation as an endangered species due to its apparent decline outside of the valley.

The high groundwater table of the valley and its extensive wetlands support interesting and varied species, but the water table is not closely connected to the Rio Grande itself. Fed primarily by mountains to the west, the Rio Grande's headwaters rise along the Continental Divide in the Weminuche and La Garita wilderness areas. Major tributaries, such as the Alamosa and Conejos rivers, drain the southern San Juan Mountains. These rivers nourish stands of cottonwood, and the combination of roosting sites and riparian habitat attracts the largest population of wintering bald eagles in Colorado — as many as 300 in some winters.

Nature Conservancy biologists have identified one exemplary stand of riparian deciduous forest near the confluence of the Conejos and Rio Grande as particularly significant. This community of narrowleaf cottonwood and coyote willow retains a diversity lacking in much of the heavily manipulated river corridor through the valley. Perhaps more dramatic in an ecological context is an expansive wetland formed by McIntire Spring, a large unspoiled wetland that Conservancy scientists call "the best of the rest."

Near the Colorado state line, the Rio Grande begins to incise its way into the lava flows that mark the southern terminus of the San Luis Valley. Several small mesas, such as Flat Top and San Luis, rise above the volcanic plain, and to their east the river cuts down through the uplifted basalt. For its last eight miles in Colorado, the Rio Grande's corridor is marked by 100- to 200-foot volcanic cliffs, the start of a much deeper and longer canyon that extends far into New Mexico.

Several serendipitous factors combine to create a spectacular habitat for raptors in this canyon of the Rio Grande. The canyon's cliffs offer innumerable nesting sites for eagles, hawks, and falcons while the surrounding sagebrush and mixed desert shrub rangeland supports an abundant rodent population. In Colorado alone, the combination of plentiful prey and nesting sites results in some 40 raptor nests, including eleven prairie falcon and four golden eagle aeries. Raptor populations in New Mexico are even greater. The Rio Grande is home to the second highest density of nesting raptors in the nation, preceded only by the renowned Birds of Prey preserve along the Snake River in Idaho.

The Rio Grande's wetlands, waterfowl populations, rare plant communities, and raptor sites underscore the intricate interactions of native ecosystems. As game and land managers are now learning, disrupting any part of this natural symbiosis requires mitigating activities — which can further disrupt ecological cycles. The farther natural cycles get out of whack, the more difficult it becomes to correct them. Efforts to preserve the habitats of native species like *Cleome* or outstanding wetlands such as McIntire Spring represent small strides in turning the corner of this counterproductive cycle.

*The Rio Grande carves through ancient lava flows in the San Luis Valley*

In 1968, Congress passed landmark legislation to preserve a few of the nation's rivers in their natural, free-flowing condition. The Wild and Scenic Rivers Act allows for the designation of certain streams containing "outstandingly remarkable" ecological, geological, historical, or other significant features in order to prevent either the inundation or the de-watering of these streams. In the mid-1970s, Congress specified that 12 Colorado rivers be studied for wild and scenic river status, among them the Conejos River in southern Colorado. After extensive study by the U.S. Forest Service, 32 miles of the Conejos were recommended for designation in order to protect the river's noteworthy scenery, trout fishing, and wildlife. Since then, federal land managers have proposed numerous other Colorado rivers for inclusion in the National Wild and Scenic Rivers System. Because of continuing objections by Colorado's water development community, Congress has unfortunately designated only one wild and scenic river in Colorado, the Cache la Poudre west of Fort Collins.

*Morning fog lifts to reveal the Conejos River, Rio Grande National Forest*

*North Clear Creek Falls, a tributary of the Rio Grande, Rio Grande National Forest*

*Pole Creek cuts through formations of eroded volcanic ash, Rio Grande National Forest*

Southwest Colorado's mountains are the result of many millions of years of extensive volcanic activity followed by glaciation and erosion. Beginning approximately 35 million years ago, successive waves of volcanic activity occurred off and on for the next 30 million years. In the initial phase, lava flows and volcanic ash covered an area more than 100 miles wide to a depth of 4,000 feet. Volcanic events continued to pour ash and lava across the landscape, culminating in flows of black basaltic lava. Pole Creek's watershed carves through an area of the San Juan Mountains covered by ash and lava flows some 29 million years ago. One common volcanic rock type found along Pole Creek is called breccia — shreds of molten rock, blown out of volcanoes, which later congealed into lumpy, angular rock. Other formations in this area consist of tuff composed of volcanic ash and cinder. Both are relatively soft and susceptible to erosion by streams.

*Beaver pond along the Alamosa River, Rio Grande National Forest*

Alamosa and Monte Vista national wildlife refuges, two of Colorado's five federal wildlife refuges, are located along the Rio Grande in the San Luis Valley. The refuges were established to compensate for the loss of natural wetlands, and today the valley is considered the most important waterfowl breeding area in Colorado. Sandhill cranes, along with several endangered whooping cranes adopted by the flock, stop over at the refuges each spring and fall during their migrations between the Gulf Coast and Canada. At the lower end of the valley on the New Mexico state line, an eight-mile stretch of the Rio Grande boasts one of the densest concentrations of raptor nests in the United States. More than 40 raptor nesting sites have been identified, including some eleven prairie falcon nests and four golden eagle aeries. Biologists believe that some nests show signs of more than 200 years of continual use.

*Sunrise along the Rio Grande as it flows through the San Luis Valley*

*Middle Fork of the Conejos River, South San Juan Wilderness*

*The beginnings of the East Fork of the Rio Chama, South San Juan Wilderness*

In 1979, the last confirmed sighting of a grizzly bear in Colorado occurred when a bow hunter killed a sow grizzly in what is now the South San Juan Wilderness. Since that time, several searches for evidence of grizzlies have been conducted, all with indefinite results. Many bear advocates believe that the South San Juans offer the most likely habitat for grizzlies in Colorado because of the area's remoteness and rugged terrain. The Colorado Division of Wildlife coordinated an unsuccessful two-year search in the early 1980s. In 1991, two conservation groups, Citizens for the Colorado Grizzly and Round River Conservation Studies, started their own grizzly surveys. While these groups have yet to uncover definitive evidence, they have recorded bear scat, apparent grizzly hairs, and one reliable sighting of a sow and three cubs.

*Sunrise above Archuleta Lake, headwaters of the South Fork of the Rio Grande, Weminuche Wilderness*

# THE SAN JUAN

## RIVER OF THE ANCIENT ONES

On August 7, 1776, fathers Silvestre Velez de Escalante and Francisco Antanasio Dominguez paused on the banks of the Rio de la Piedra Parada in what is today extreme southern Colorado. They had left Santa Fe just ten days earlier on what would turn into an epic five-month journey through western Colorado, Utah, and northern New Mexico. Though several Spanish explorers had previously passed through the area, it was still largely an unknown wilderness to Europeans. As the fathers explored deeper into this uncharted land, they discovered remains of long-since vanished civilizations that in many ways rivaled those of contemporary Europe. Near the Dolores River, the expedition found extensive ruins that today bear Escalante's name.

Dominguez and Escalante, as well as numerous other Spanish explorers, traversed much of this region long before more familiar American frontiersmen, such as Zebulon Pike and John Fremont. The 17th- and 18th-century Spanish adventurers discovered the remnants of two Anasazi cultures: the Northern, or Mesa Verde, Anasazi, and the Chaco Anasazi of the San Juan basin. These civilizations were marked by scattered villages, a far-flung network of roads, and intensive agricultural practices that included water diversions and irrigation. With many communities of several thousand individuals or more, the flourishing Anasazi culture supported populations similar to present-day communities in the Four Corners.

Southwestern Colorado has an illustrious history of human habitation and complex cultures. The best-known Anasazi ruins in Mesa Verde National Park compare favorably in grandeur with the majestic castles of Europe. For hundreds of years, the Anasazi and their predecessors built towns, conducted commerce, and developed agriculture here, yet today this corner of the state is by many accounts the wildest and least manipulated of any area in Colorado. This seems to be an apparent contradiction: a populated area existing side-by-side with unspoiled wilderness.

Looking at a map of Colorado's rivers, southwestern Colorado has a unique peculiarity of topography. Most river drainages branch out symmetrically like tree limbs. But in the San Juan River drainage, a half-dozen rivers shoot arrow-straight out of the San Juan Mountains toward the New Mexico line and the San Juan River. The San Juan and its tributaries — the Piedra, Los Pinos, Florida, Animas, La Plata, and Mancos — are fed by the vast snowpacks of the San Juan Mountains, snow that accumulates in the glacier-carved cirques and bowls along the Continental Divide. Surging snowmelt rushes through the area's overlying volcanics into the lower sedimentary formations of the San Juan basin. In this fashion, the San Juan and its tributaries act like Colorado's other rivers in that they exhibit peak spring runoff. The rivers of the San Juan Mountains confound this traditional pattern, however, with a late summer streamflow peak resulting from summer monsoons. August and September bring drenching rainstorms fueled by moisture from the Gulf of Mexico. On rivers like the Piedra — called the "river of the standing rock" by Dominguez and Escalante — the highest recorded flows occurred in September, the result of thunderstorms in the San Juans.

Evidence of ancient civilization exists with modern-day wilderness along the Piedra. One of the most northerly outposts of the Chacoan Anasazi is located on a promontory called Chimney Rock that juts above the Piedra south of Highway 160. Some have called Chimney Rock the Machu Picchu of the United States because of its commanding views of the Piedra River Valley and the San Juan Mountains. At 7,600 feet in elevation, it is unmistakably the highest-elevation pre-Columbian architecture in North America. The site consists of approximately 90 ruins, including several large Chacoan-style kivas as well as structures built in the Mesa Verde style.

The Chacoan Anasazi civilization was centered in Chaco Canyon in northern New Mexico. During its pinnacle, around 1100 A.D., Chaco Canyon served as the hub of an extensive trading network. People from surrounding communities traveled there to trade goods and acquire turquoise. Some archaeologists believe that Chaco Canyon eventually attained religious significance because of its importance as a center of commerce. Chimney Rock represented the extreme northern extension of the Chacoan Anasazi, and its location high atop a promontory has prompted some researchers to assign religious significance to it as well. Others include it among a number of sites believed to have served as a scattered eastern defensive perimeter for the Chacoan system.

Chimney Rock lies amidst a ponderosa pine forest that covers the lower reaches of the Piedra. Naturally functioning ponderosa pine forests represent one of the most threatened woodland ecosystems in Colorado. Because of their low elevation and considerable aesthetic qualities, ponderosa pine forests have felt the impact of human settlements. *(Continued on page 58)*

---

*The San Juan River, Southern Ute Indian Reservation*
*Overleaf: Headwaters of Vallecito Creek, a tributary of the San Juan River, Weminuche Wilderness*

These forests depend on frequent, low-intensity fires to maintain themselves. Because of human occupation, land managers aggressively suppress forest fires, which permits understory species such as white fir to prosper. When fires do occur, the immature fir trees provide ladder fuels that propel ground fires toward the forest canopy. The result can be devastating crown fires that obliterate the old-growth ponderosa pine forests, one of the reasons that old-growth forests (those with trees 150 years or older) are increasingly hard to find.

The southern reaches of the San Juans, and the Piedra drainage in particular, include some of the most abundant and least modified ponderosa pine forests in Colorado. Perhaps 40,000 acres of ponderosa pine remain in the San Juan National Forest. Of these, 8,000 acres lie within a single roadless, virgin forest in the Piedra watershed. This area offers an excellent opportunity for restoring the natural fire cycles needed by ponderosa pine forests to achieve old-growth ecosystems. Only in a wilderness setting, far from human habitation and in areas withdrawn from timber-harvesting activities, can managers experiment with let-burn policies aimed at restoring the natural, low-intensity ground fires needed to perpetuate the vanishing ponderosa pine ecosystem.

The Navajo River, another San Juan tributary, emphasizes the basin's wild nature. The Navajo people called it *Powuska*, meaning Mad River, out of respect for its schizophrenic behavior — rampaging spring floods and late summer droughts. The Navajo drains an area that many consider to be Colorado's most remote wilderness: the South San Juans. It was near the Navajo's headwaters that Colorado's last confirmed grizzly bear was killed in 1979 by a bow hunter. Some believe a remnant grizzly population still survives in the Navajo drainage.

The Colorado Division of Wildlife conducted a fruitless search of the area for grizzlies in the early 1980s. In 1991 two citizens groups continued the effort and again began looking for grizzlies. While the searchers believe they have found grizzly bear scat, and some area ranchers reported sightings of a sow with cubs, no definitive evidence of habitation yet exists. The U.S. Fish and Wildlife Service, the agency charged with recovery of grizzlies, lists the San Juans as their southernmost potential habitat, whether for recovery or reintroduction of the species, which is endangered in the lower 48 states. That an area populated by humans for more than a thousand years could still harbor the fiercest North American predator bodes well for the future coexistence of humans and other native animal species.

The vanished civilizations of the San Juan watershed suggest the powerful restorative powers of nature. It is hard to imagine that a society comprised of towns and villages populated by thousands of individuals could largely disappear in the brief time span of 500 years. Mayan and Aztec ruins of similar age vanished into the dense jungles of Central America, but for evidence of an extensive society in the arid Southwest to fade as well offers hope for nature's inherent healing abilities. Evenutally the fields and agricultural systems of the Anasazi were overtaken by forests of pinyon and juniper.

While we will never know the Anasazi's impact on native plant and animal communities, the fact that the forests returned and thrived in the absence of human disturbance suggests that our similarly disturbed modern environments can be reclaimed, with one caveat well put by pioneer ecologist Aldo Leopold: "The first principle of intelligent tinkering is to save all the parts." If we have truly saved all of the parts of the San Juan River ecosystem through farsighted legislation like the Endangered Species Act, or through swift intervention in preserving biologically rich but threatened native habitats, then the future of the river is bright indeed.

*The Piedra River, a tributary of the San Juan River, cuts through canyons of pine, spruce, and fir, San Juan National Forest*

*Boulder-strewn banks of the Piedra River, Second Box Canyon, San Juan National Forest*

One of Colorado's most threatened forest ecosystems is the ponderosa pine forest. Human settlement occurs pervasively throughout these forests because of their aesthetic quality and because the trees grow on lower elevation foothills accessible to development. Old-growth ponderosa pine forests (those with trees 150 years or older) depend on relatively frequent, low-intensity fires that burn undergrowth but do not spread to the forest canopy. This fire ecology creates the open, park-like setting of pondersa pine forests. Extensive development and the fear of property loss, however, precludes the natural fire regime. Some of Colorado's most abundant and least modified pondersa pine forests, more than 8,000 acres, are found in the Piedra River drainage.

*Aptly named Cascade Creek feeds into the Animas River, San Juan National Forest*

Autumn brings colorful displays to Colorado's valleys and high country. But why do trees turn yellow and red in the fall? With shorter daylight hours, leaves cease producing chlorophyll. Chlorophyll absorbs red and blue wavelengths of light, reflecting primarily the green portion of the color spectrum — which explains why leaves are green. Other pigments, such as yellowish carotenes and xanthophylls and reddish anthocyanins, are also present in leaves but are normally masked by chlorophyll. As leaves stop producing chlorophyll, carotenes and xanthophylls dominate, turning the leaves yellow. Some species increase production of anthocyanin as chlorophyll diminishes, and in these bushes and trees the leaves take on a bright red appearance. The aesthetic consequence for Colorado nature lovers comes in the shimmering yellows and oranges of aspen trees, golden cottonwoods, and dazzling red oakbrush.

*Early autumn along the San Juan River, Southern Ute Indian Reservation*

*Headwaters of Vallecito Creek, Sunlight Creek descends from Sunlight Peak,
elevation 14,059 feet, Weminuche Wilderness*

*The Animas River, a tributary of the San Juan River, originates in
heavily mined mountains near Silverton*

*Winter waterfalls on the La Plata River, a tributary of the San Juan River, San Juan National Forest*

Many Colorado rivers originate on national forest lands that have been designated as wilderness areas. Under the Wilderness Act, Congress can set aside roadless areas that retain their "primeval character and influence" and where "man himself is a visitor who does not remain." Motorized vehicles are prohibited in these areas, as are development activities, such as logging and mining. Since the Wilderness Act was passed in 1964, 2.6 million acres have been designated as wilderness in Colorado. Although this may seem significant, it amounts to less than four percent of Colorado's land area. Legislation now pending would add another 600,000 acres. Colorado's largest wilderness area, the Weminuche Wilderness, encompasses almost 500,000 acres in the San Juan Mountains, including the headwaters of several major rivers — the Rio Grande, the San Juan, and the Animas.

*Alpine tarn at 12,500 feet, headwaters of Vallecito Creek, Weminuche Wilderness*

*Lime Creek feeds into Cascade Creek, which in turn feeds the Animas River*
*Overleaf: Pinon, juniper, cottonwood, and scrub oak line the banks of the San Juan River,*
*Southern Ute Indian Reservation*

*Vallecito Creek, the central southern drainage of the Weminuche Wilderness*

*The Navajo River, a tributary of the San Juan River, Tierra Amarilla Grant*

# THE DOLORES

## JOURNEY INTO THE DESERT

As is common in the Colorado Rockies, spring comes abruptly to the San Juan Mountains, and floating the Dolores means catching the wave of surging snowmelt in late April and May. At 7,000 feet, spring mornings are crisp. Awakening rafters wearily roll out of sleeping bags, dress quickly, and stamp feet and rub hands while waiting for coffee water to boil. Because many arrived at the boat launch late the previous night, the morning sun reveals a disheveled scene of gear and bedrolls scattered haphazardly across the landscape, more reminiscent of a Civil War battlefield than a boat launch.

Dolores River journeys typically begin at a river crossing called Bradfield Bridge, which lies midway between the river's craggy, alpine headwaters in the San Juans and Disappointment Valley in the Colorado desert. The river cuts a steep though shallow canyon into surrounding benchlands. Thickets of Gambel oak clog the hillsides, and at the boat launch only the occasional ponderosa pine hints at the botanical delights waiting just downstream. The Dolores is swift and clear here, and its shallows reveal brightly colored red sandstone boulders mixed among the granites and volcanics transported from higher in the watershed.

Find a group of diehard river rats in western Colorado, and the conversation will undoubtedly turn to the Dolores River. Rafters hold a special place in their hearts for the Dolores, which provides Colorado's longest, wildest, and, by many accounts, most beautiful river trip, a scenic palette of yellow-barked ponderosa pines and sheer red rock canyon walls. Within minutes of casting off from the Bradfield Bridge launch into the quickening current, rafters catch sight of stately ponderosas along the riverbanks. Soon the canyon cuts deeper into red walls of Wingate sandstone. Spring often brings chilling rainstorms, but once the storms have passed, they leave behind bright green foliage framed by glistening sandstone cliffs. This first night on the river, rafters look forward to camping amidst towering ponderosa pines. Ramrod straight, the trees reach skyward, their trunks so large it takes two people linking arms to encircle one solitary giant.

Around midday on day two of the trip, boaters pass the Cahone pumping station at the Dolores's momentous U-turn. Here, after feinting in a southwesterly direction toward the San Juan River, the Dolores turns and sweeps north for 100 miles to its confluence with the Colorado River, upstream of Moab, Utah. The bend marks a turn-

ing point for the river in other ways as well. Downstream, the river drops into ever drier and more desolate country, finally carving a thousand-foot-deep red rock gorge as it nears the state line. The surrounding walls climb upward and outward, and the canyon's scale begins to take on a Grand Canyon-like quality. Soon the rafters' attention is drawn to a more immediate concern — the treacherous waters of Snaggletooth Rapid.

The Dolores is small in comparison to many western desert rivers, and its rapids are narrow and choked with boulders. One of these, a particularly menacing jagged point, gives Snaggletooth its name. The current slows and the river pools above the rapid. Approaching the bank, rowers quickly stroke for the overhanging oakbrush that marks the scouting point. Boats secured, passengers and boatmen alike scamper along the riverbank for a glimpse of Snaggletooth.

From shore, they scout their route through the rapid, attempting to gauge the push and spin of the water as it drops and swirls over and around both hidden and conspicuous obstacles. At the rapid's entrance, a narrow, boulder-free channel lures rafters to a cascading ledge. Rafts then drop over the ledge, in springtime filled with water, and careen ever so close to the threatening visage of Snaggletooth rock. Some rafts bounce nose-first off the rock; the unlucky few wrap round it like cellophane. After watching several boats make the hazardous journey with varying degrees of success, rafting parties are often tempted to use the jeep road that parallels the rapid to haul their gear around the maelstrom of angry water.

Snaggletooth Rapid becomes impassable when the river's flow falls below 800 cubic feet per second. The rocks are exposed and the current is insufficient to safely navigate rafts through the obstacles. Irrigation withdrawals upstream near the town of Dolores have long depleted the river. With the completion of the Bureau of Reclamation's McPhee Reservoir in 1984, the problem was exacerbated. Because of miscalculations, however, much of the impounded water is no longer wanted by local farmers, and water from the reservoir may soon become available for release downstream.

McPhee Reservoir and the associated Dolores Project experienced unanticipated cost overruns to the degree that the project, originally estimated to cost $50 million, ended up with a price tag closer to $570 million. Consequently, the price charged to farmers for irrigation water was so high that several dozen farmers asked out of

*Sunrise above the Dolores River, Dolores River Canyon BLM Wilderness Study Area*

the project. Similarly, projected population increases failed to materialize for the nearby town of Cortez, leaving it with more water than needed. The availability of this unwanted irrigation and municipal water opens the possibility for additional downstream water releases for rafting, as well as for the late season flows needed to maintain a growing trout fishery. Federal river managers have also identified the need for large flushing flows, several thousand cubic feet per second, every other year to mimic natural spring runoff. This would restore channel features, such as sandbars, required for healthy riparian plant communities. Excess reservoir water and the pressing need for downstream releases may well provide opportunities for new and innovative methods of securing higher streamflows.

With Snaggletooth Rapid safely behind and the complexities of water management farthest from their thoughts, rafters enter the cathedral-like environs of Slickrock Canyon on the third or fourth day. In *The Rivers of Colorado*, author Jeff Rennicke calls this stretch of river Little Glen Canyon, a remembrance of the renowned canyon flooded by Lake Powell and the Glen Canyon Dam. Upstream, where Disappointment Creek oozes into the Dolores, the river turns the color and consistency of a chocolate milkshake. There, desert seeps line the banks and issue a tepid, musty smell that gives the area the moniker "stinking desert." But here, in the tranquil confines of Slickrock Canyon, where vertical red walls rise from the river's edge, the sweet fragrance of clear springs and deep plunge pools characterize the sculpted side canyons. The river's lazy current barely gurgles, occasionally sweeping boats under soaring alcoves of overhanging rock or the arching limbs of box elder. A fine wilderness, many might think, and indeed the canyon and 30,000 acres of surrounding mesas are proposed for wilderness designation by the Bureau of Land Management. One particularly alluring tributary, Spring Creek, entices boaters to delay and explore. After the blazing desert sun and dry heat, rafters are soothed by the humidity of this cool, shady refuge.

Moisture makes its way through the seemingly impenetrable sandstone strata and seeps to the surface through fractures and porous layers in the canyon walls. Water weakens the rock and great slabs peel off, creating concave alcoves. As the water evaporates, it leaves behind dissolved salts in white abstract patterns that testify to the presence of both wet and dormant seeps.

Maidenhair ferns droop from the rock walls, and dense grasses carpet sandy slopes below these hanging gardens. The brief, fierce action of flash floods thundering down from overhanging lips has scoured depressions in the solid sandstone and left pools of varying clarity and depth. Green moss garnishes the pools, and water striders crazily skitter across their surface. Tadpoles slumber in undisturbed silt, scooting out of harm's way as an alien hand reaches down to snare them. From this remote sanctuary, the river is but a silent whisper, and the roar of Spring Creek Rapid is quickly lost in the canyon's labyrinth of twists and bends.

Back on the river, as the Dolores drops deeper into the bowels of Slickrock Canyon, blinding white Navajo sandstone makes its appearance far above the red Wingate. The eye is drawn upward to where Douglas fir trees grasp tenuously to almost-vertical walls. Dense green foliage, brilliant bands of white sandstone, vibrant red walls, and piercing blue skies — only the river itself is drab and olive-green, its pulsating life transmitted through the undulating motion of the raft. Its serenity encourages one to forget time, and with little thought one could float another 200 miles to the Colorado River and beyond to Lake Powell. But as is always the case, civilization beckons once again, and around the next bend the Bedrock boat ramp signals the end of another river sojourn.

*Spring greenery along the San Miguel River, a tributary of the Dolores River protected as The Nature Conservancy's San Miguel Canyon Preserve*

The Galloping Geese of the Rio Grande Southern Railroad filled a colorful chapter in Colorado railroad history. A motor car converted to rail to carry freight, mail, and passengers with a one-man crew, the first Galloping Goose was born in 1931 out of the need to cut expenses along low-trafficked routes on the bankrupt Rio Grande Southern. Soon, seven Geese were constructed in the railroad's Ridgway shop, first from Buick truck bodies and later using Pierce-Arrow bodies and parts. The eye-catching hybrids looked like elongated delivery trucks on rails. According to railroad historian Mallory Hope Ferrell, the term "Galloping Goose" was coined from the goose-like honk of their horns or because of their waddling gait on uneven tracks. From 1931 until the railroad's demise in 1951, the Geese ran regularly between the towns of Ridgway, Telluride, Durango, and Dolores. Several Geese are still on display in Dolores, Rico, and Telluride.

*The West Dolores River, San Juan National Forest*

*Sandstone boulders at mid-river, Dolores River*
*Overleaf: Late afternoon light on the Dolores River, Dolores River Canyon BLM Wilderness Study Area*

Thirty thousand acres of the Dolores River Canyon between Slickrock and Bedrock have been proposed by the Bureau of Land Management (BLM) for wilderness designation. The Dolores is one of some 50 areas, totalling 800,000 acres, that the BLM has reviewed for potential wilderness status since 1976. The BLM completed its studies in 1991 and proposed to Congress approximately 400,000 acres for wilderness designation. These BLM areas consist largely of lower-elevation deserts, mesas, and canyons that will add substantially to the ecological diversity of existing wilderness areas, which are mostly alpine and forest ecosystems. Significant downstream portions of most major Colorado rivers flow through proposed BLM wilderness areas. In addition to the Dolores, other areas include the Colorado River through Ruby Canyon near the Utah state line, Cross Mountain Canyon on the Yampa, Gunnison Gorge below the Black Canyon of the Gunnison, Browns Canyon on the Arkansas, and the Rio Grande at the New Mexico state line.

*Sandstone seep high above the Dolores River, Dolores River Canyon BLM Wilderness Study Area*

Snaggletooth Rapid was first run in 1948 by Doc Marston, although "run" may be too strong a verb. Like many a wary boater since, Marston wisely decided to portage his wooden boats and gear around the rapid before continuing downstream. Casual observers of river running may wonder how maelstroms like Snaggletooth are ever successfully navigated. Whitewater rafters and kayakers approach all such rapids with great respect and pull in to shore above each rapid to scout it first. Boaters gauge the direction of the current and frequently pick a route down the V-wave, the smooth tongue of water that marks the path of least resistance. This tongue can be deceptive at times, however, and can sweep the unsuspecting toward jagged rocks or barely submerged boulders. Rafters use oars and paddles to direct themselves away from the greatest obstacles, all the while attempting to read the push and pull of the current so as to minimize their own work.

*Snaggletooth Rapid, rated Class IV, the most challenging whitewater on the Dolores River*

Three segments of the San Miguel River have been incorporated into a riparian preserve by The Nature Conservancy. Encompassing 605 acres and six miles of riverfront, these three sections protect excellent examples of several globally rare riparian plant communities. The South Fork Miguel Preserve, located ten miles downstream from Telluride, protects a prime example of a Colorado blue spruce and black twinberry community. The San Miguel Canyon Preserve, four miles downstream from Placerville, maintains a narrowleaf cottonwood, Colorado blue spruce, and thinleaf alder community. The lower preserve, near the confluence of Tabeguache Creek near Uravan, harbors riparian communities of Rio Grande cottonwood, skunkbush, sumac, and coyote willow. The San Miguel is a relatively short river but is virtually unaltered by impoundments. These preserves provide a significant start toward safeguarding the natural features of the San Miguel.

*Ponderosa pines along the Dolores River, below McPhee Reservoir*

*Melting spring snows on Sunshine Mountain feed the headwaters of the San Miguel River, as seen from the The Nature Conservancy's South Fork San Miguel Preserve*

# THE GUNNISON

## INNOVATIVE ACTION AND INSTREAM FLOWS

"Unbelievable. Last Friday on the upper Taylor River, I caught a 29-inch rainbow, weighing over 12 pounds, on a fly that measured a 64th of an inch. Three-pound test. Every fisherman's dream," gloated Hank Hotze, proprietor of Gunnison River Expeditions, as he gazed at a photograph of this remarkable fish. "From a fishery point of view, the Gunnison basin is without peer."

Hank Hotze fished the Gunnison's headwaters that day, but it is the lower Gunnison, below the Black Canyon of the Gunnison National Monument, where the river carves a 13-mile canyon called Gunnison Gorge, that Hotze knows best. He is arguably the leading authority on this stretch of the river, a status gained from guiding several thousand fishermen through the area since 1981. When asked to expound on the Gunnison Gorge's superlative fishing, Hotze doesn't take much prodding to make his fish story more believable.

"First and foremost, it's difficult to get to. Secondly, the quality of the ecosystem as it relates to food, water temperature, and habitat creates an absolutely perfect environment to grow trophy fish. You can't catch 24-inch rainbows hardly anywhere in the West, but the Gunnison provides them in droves.

"The Gunnison has more big fish per mile than any other stream in Colorado," Hotze continues. When he says big fish, he means it. The Gunnison Gorge has more than 650 trout per mile greater than 16 inches in length and weighing more than two pounds. He attributes this to abundant food sources, such as stoneflies, that supply trout with high-protein nutrients.

Hotze's clients may take four days to float the 13-mile Gunnison Gorge. At this rate, one could leisurely stroll through the canyon if it weren't for frequent impassable cliffs. But with Hotze and his clients lollygagging at every eddy, hole, and riffle, the miles simply don't pass very quickly. Hotze plays the part of a stern parent on these trips, rousing his charges from warm sleeping bags in the faint light of dawn and herding them toward sure-fire trout habitat. Guests make up for this early morning fishing extravaganza with a required afternoon siesta. At dusk, Hotze once again deposits them at guaranteed trout holes. Even rank amateurs pull in 20 to 30 fish per day, which Hotze has them release.

The Gunnison's extraordinary productivity is all the more remarkable given the environmental insults to which it is regularly subjected. "The Gunnison is the most resilient river I've ever seen," Hotze remarks. "We

normally get heavy August rains that dump unbelievable amounts of water on the highly erosive soils east of Ute Park. This clogs the river and spawning areas with silt, but as long as the river has flushing flows, it can survive."

And resilient the Gunnison must be, for it is one of Colorado's hardest-working rivers. A huge agricultural diversion began in 1909 with the completion of the Gunnison Tunnel. Diverting upwards of 1,100 cubic feet per second (cfs), the tunnel annually takes more than 300,000 acre-feet out of the Gunnison River, channeling it into the Uncompahgre Valley to irrigate farmlands around Montrose and Delta. This diversion removes one-third of the Gunnison's yearly volume, equivalent to the water needed to supply the municipal needs of more than a million people.

Four large dams now constrain the Gunnison and its tributaries. The first, Taylor Park Reservoir, was constructed in 1939 to provide high-elevation storage of agricultural water for later release to farmers in the Uncompahgre Valley. In the 1960s and 1970s, the three dams of the Wayne Aspinall Unit of the Colorado River Storage Project were constructed, including the massive Blue Mesa Reservoir. These dams are commonly referred to as cash register dams because one of their purposes is to generate money through hydroelectricity sales to pay off the construction costs of reclamation projects throughout the Colorado River basin.

Before the dams, the Gunnison had a reputation as a fierce trout river. Years later, as expert fishermen like Hotze attest, it still possesses enough of the latent attributes of healthy stream biology to produce renowned fishing. It was against this framework that The Nature Conservancy hatched an innovative technique for preserving the Gunnison's natural ecology.

The Conservancy operates in the private marketplace, purchasing properties containing rare or significant ecosystems, thereby safeguarding them for future generations. In the early 1970s, longtime Conservancy board member David Harrison made a small but natural leap in the evolution of the organization's thinking. As a western water attorney, he was intimately familiar with the administration of water rights. Since water rights are considered property, Harrison thought, why not translate the Conservancy's successes in land-based property acquisitions to include water-based property? And what better place to attempt this than on the Gunnison River through Gunnison Gorge. *(Continued on page 88)*

---

*The Gunnison River carves through Gunnison Gorge BLM Wilderness Study Area*
*Overleaf: White Rock Mountain reflected in the headwaters of Copper Creek,*
*Maroon Bells-Snowmass Wilderness*

The idea started slowly, but moved into high gear when Harrison took a trip through the Gunnison Gorge with the president of Pittsburg and Midway Coal Mining Company. The company owned a conditional water right for a reservoir at the mouth of Gunnison Gorge. A conditional water right is one that has never been developed but is still recognized by Colorado water courts as sort of a "first dibs" on dam construction. After seeing the extraordinary natural values of the Gunnison, Pittsburg and Midway reassessed its development plans, and in 1987 the company donated its water right to the Conservancy.

The Conservancy, in turn, hoped to convert the conditional reservoir right into an actual 300-cfs instream flow right. Instream flow is the minimum amount of water necessary to sustain the natural ecology of a river. Obtaining instream flow rights in the Gunnison Gorge would give The Nature Conservancy legal standing in water rights administration. Under a state law passed in 1973, however, only the Colorado Water Conservation Board can file water rights to maintain instream flow.

Water rights are based on the concept of "first in time, first in right," meaning that those with the oldest water rights have the highest priority. Because nearly all the water in Colorado rivers and streams has already been claimed, at least conditionally, downstream water rights filed by the water conservation board are often junior to more senior, conditional rights upstream.

"The main benefit of acquiring a water right like this is that it results in better seniority," says Robert Wigington, the Conservancy water attorney who handled the Pittsburg and Midway donation. "It gives a better priority position, which is key to the value of any water right." The water right donated to the Conservancy by Pittsburg and Midway dates from the 1960s, which placed it ahead of several new proposed diversions. But because under state law only the water conservation board can own this kind of instream flow right, the Conservancy needed to donate the right to the state.

At this point the going got sticky. Some Colorado water users objected to the idea of converting a conditional right into an absolute right for minimum streamflows, even though conditional rights were often converted into water rights for other purposes. Because of the contentious nature of this donation, Wigington negotiated management agreements with the municipal and agricultural water users who would be affected, and, after several years of intensive negotiations, he con-

vinced the state to accept the donation. In doing so, the state water board crossed a new policy frontier by accepting the concept of converting a senior conditional water right to an instream flow right.

While the state consented to the donation and its policy implications, some of Colorado's established water community continued to object. After accepting the donation, the water conservation board needed to change the conditional reservoir right to an instream flow right, which required action by Colorado's water court system. The state filed for the change in use, but several municipalities and water districts from Colorado's Front Range opposed it. It now appears that the long-range policy implications of the donation will ultimately be decided by the Colorado Supreme Court.

Diverting one-third of a river's water out of its channel, immense federal hydroelectric dams, arcane legal arguments about conditional versus absolute water rights — all of these issues highlight the intricately complex nature of Colorado water law and the Gunnison's water rights. What sometimes gets lost in the shuffle is the very real needs of the river.

Stream biologists view 300 cfs as a good start at setting a firm foundation for base flows in the river. But some observers, like Hotze, believe more water is needed at certain times. According to Hotze, the measure of "enough" is a river full to its banks at critical times of the year. And, says Hotze in a metaphysical moment, the river itself has participated in many of the decisions affecting it. "In the past, when summer thunderstorms poured loads of silt into the river and the low streamflow was unable to clear the trout spawning beds, the river fought back by choking with silt and killing fish. But when flows returned to acceptable levels, the number of fish doubled. It was as if the river was saying, 'Hey, this is what you get when you give me water, you get the most unbelievable fishing.'"

According to Hotze, every time the river has been threatened, it has spoken one way or another. We can only hope the Gunnison continues to speak. And for those unable to hear its words, we will have to rely on interpreters like Hank Hotze.

*Henson Creek plunges through narrow cliffs on its way toward the Lake Fork of the Gunnison River, near Lake City*

The Lake Fork of the Gunnison, one of the Gunnison River's largest tributaries, drains the northern slopes of the San Juan Mountains. The confluence is now buried beneath Blue Mesa Reservoir, but in the winter of 1874, the two forks of the Gunnison confused a party of six men attempting to travel east from what is now Montrose to the trading post at Saguache. The party mistakenly concluded that the Lake Fork was the main stem of Gunnison and veered south, and ever deeper, into the heart of the San Juans. Perhaps realizing their error, or because of heavy snows, the men stopped at the foot of a broad alpine plateau. Only one of the group was ever heard from again, and Alferd Packer's grisly tale earned him notoriety in Colorado history books. His companions met their fates just upstream of Lake City on the flank of aptly named Cannibal Plateau.

*Canyon Creek, a tributary of the Uncompahgre River, Uncompahgre National Forest*

*Lake Fork of the Gunnison River, Gunnison National Forest*

One of the few remaining big dam proposal sites in Colorado is located along the Gunnison River at Dominguez Canyon. First proposed by the Bureau of Reclamation in the 1970s, the idea was abandoned because of its poor cost-benefit ratio. A private consortium resurrected the dam proposal in 1986. As envisioned by its proponents, Dominguez Dam would inundate 30 miles of the Gunnison River, including the lower reaches of Dominguez Creek. Dam proponents face several major obstacles, not the least of which is finding a market for the water. They have suggested selling the water to southern California or using it to generate hydroelectricity. Proponents must also overcome objections from government agencies and environmental groups, for the dam would destroy the proposed Dominguez Canyon Wilderness Area and negatively impact several species of endangered fish in the Gunnison and Colorado rivers.

*The Gunnison River, Gunnison Gorge BLM Wilderness Study Area*

*Early spring along Dominguez Creek, Dominguez Canyon BLM Wilderness Study Area*
*Overleaf: Marsh marigolds, Peeler Basin, headwaters of the Slate River*

*Falls below Lake Irwin, Ruby Anthracite Creek, headwaters of the North Fork of the Gunnison River*

*Snowmelt from the Beckwith Mountains feeds Ruby Anthracite Creek, Horse Ranch Park,*
*Gunnison National Forest*

# THE COLORADO

## A SENSE OF PLACE

For 40 years, visitors entering Grand Junction from the south via Highway 50 gained their first impressions of the community from expansive automobile junkyards and associated industrial flotsam. As the highway dropped off Orchard Mesa and crossed the Colorado River, these junkyards stretched upstream and down, burying the riverbanks under scrap metal, worn tires, and abandoned mobile homes.

But beginning in 1986, a remarkable transformation occurred as Grand Junction residents reclaimed their river, and with it a fair measure of civic pride. The city's river restoration marked the genesis of a larger movement along the Colorado to reconnect human settlements with the beauty of the land. It is a connection that author Wendell Berry expounded upon in an essay entitled "The Regional Motive," in which he wrote: "Without a complex knowledge of one's place, and without the faithfulness to one's place on which such knowledge depends, it is inevitable that the place will be used carelessly, and eventually destroyed."

During the 1940s and 1950s, Grand Junction's automobile junkyards were viewed as cheap flood control. When the Colorado River flooded, as it was wont to do, the river's flat banks in the Grand Valley were inundated with water for hundreds of feet on either side of the river channel. Car bodies dumped along the riverbank simply filled with silt, settled deeper into the ground, and offered better protection from the next flood.

By 1986, the sorry state of Grand Junction's southern entrance was widely recognized as a detriment, but it took a handful of Grand Junction Lions Club members to initiate action. The club traditionally donated thousands of dollars to numerous community improvement projects. While brainstorming potential projects, several members struck on the idea of improving the city's southern entrance by cleaning up a junkyard and creating a greenbelt. Led by Brian Mahoney, Lions Club members sought acquisition of 24-acre Watson's Island as well as land on the adjacent riverbank. After three years of painstaking negotiations, a deal was struck and the property purchased with $100,000 donated by the Lions Club, a $150,000 contribution from the City of Grand Junction, and $200,000 from the state's energy impact assistance fund.

Simultaneously with the Lions Club's efforts, another Grand Junction civic organization pursued its own vision for the Colorado River. Several miles downstream of Watson's Island, Helen Traylor, a spry grandmother and president of the local Audubon Society, spearheaded construction of a 1.2-mile nature trail called, appropriately enough, the Audubon Trail. In the spirit of cooperation, the Redlands Water and Power Company, Whitewater Building Materials, and other landowners donated rights-of-way for the trail along the Redlands Canal. A rough trail was soon completed with volunteer labor and materials. It was an immediate hit with valley residents.

From these initial successes, interest in the river grew. "We realized this could be a great project with expanded horizons," Mahoney recalls. A raft trip was organized for city and county officials, who marveled at the wildness of the river, even through the heart of the valley's industrial area. In no time, a joint riverfront commission was established by the City of Grand Junction and Mesa County. Its charge was to clean up the river, construct a trail system, and provide public access to this newly rediscovered natural resource.

"The riverfront commission's original charter stated that one goal was to focus community pride," says Mahoney. And focus it certainly did. Volunteers contributed 20,000 hours of labor to clean up Watson's Island, removing thousands of tires, several dozen dump-truck loads of scrap metal, and even derelict mobile homes. Building on the success of Watson's Island, the city combined with the federal government and a local charitable organization to raise $1.2 million to purchase another major junkyard downstream.

"Cleaning up Watson's Island and building a little piece of trail got everyone's attention. That turned into an idea for a river park stretching all the way from DeBeque to Loma," said Mahoney. The river park idea blossomed into a grandiose plan for 30 miles of trails (with ten miles already constructed by 1993) and interconnected state and local parks. The state approved creation of a Colorado River State Park in 1991 and acquired Corn Lake as the first section. Once the U.S. Department of Energy completes remediation of a 128-acre uranium mill-tailings pile near Grand Junction, the Division of State Parks and Outdoor Recreation will convert it into a riverbank park. The park division is also negotiating for trail easements along the river.

Mahoney's and Grand Junction's success in reclaiming community pride in their river marked the start of a revolution of sorts. Glenwood Springs, upstream of Grand Junction, got religion about rivers soon thereafter. Glenwood Springs's city council appointed a river commission and charged it with many of the same goals as that

---

*Geneva Creek, headwaters of the Crystal River, a tributary of the Roaring Fork River,*
*Maroon Bells-Snowmass Wilderness*

of Grand Junction's — cleanup, restoration, public access, and recreation. The commission laid out a master plan for eight miles of trails and initiated action to improve or create three new parks, two on the Fryingpan River and one on the Colorado.

These cooperative efforts within the Colorado River drainage belie the stubborn historical conflict between residents on the western slope of the Continental Divide and those on the eastern slope. Metropolitan Denver and Front Range communities rely heavily on the Colorado River to supply municipal water needs. Including agricultural uses, Colorado's Front Range diverts almost 500,000 acre-feet of water annually through tunnels under the divide.

For many Coloradans, the Colorado River is little more than a giant faucet, ever ready to meet the needs of sugar-beet farmers or burgeoning suburbs. But for the residents of Kremmling, Burns, McCoy, Glenwood Springs, Grand Junction, and the other communities along the river, the Colorado is much more than a water supply for distant consumers: It is their backyard and the link that connects them culturally as well as hydrologically. A visionary planning effort for the upper Colorado River offers evidence of growing recognition of this link.

As ambitious as Grand Junction's accomplishments might be, the Upper Colorado Alliance, the brainchild of Bureau of Land Management (BLM) managers in Kremmling and Glenwood Springs, may have it beat. "The Colorado is more than a locally significant resource, it is a national resource too," says Kate Kitchell, BLM manager for the Kremmling Resource Area. Kitchell believes that, in addition to the Colorado's economic worth, the natural and aesthetic values of the river also need to be recognized. In 1992, Kitchell and the BLM embarked on a cooperative effort to create a long-term vision for the Colorado, from its headwaters in Rocky Mountain National Park to Glenwood Springs, 100 miles downstream. The plan involves federal agencies, state and local governments, landowners, and special interest groups in a process intended to maximize public and private benefits while minimizing conflicts over resource use. Kitchell sees it as a public-private symbiosis.

Kitchell may be among the first land managers to apply an ecosystem approach — planning for complete watersheds by crossing jurisdictional boundaries — to manage a critical resource. The Alliance's multi-resource agenda includes improving riparian habitats, enhancing and diversifying recreation, assessing the conflicts between big game populations and private land ownership, considering the impact of public access, and maintaining water levels for recreational use. The importance of agricultural areas as open space and the economic and aesthetic value of that open space are other key issues. An immediate benefit of the Alliance's efforts was greater recognition of the river as a community resource and increased dialogue and trust among all players.

One of those involved was Grand County's planning director, Lurline Underbrink-Curran. Grand County was interested in the Alliance's ability to provide economic benefits to the Kremmling area, which relied heavily upon agriculture and logging. With the closure of the Louisiana-Pacific sawmill in 1992, Kremmling needed a diversified economy that included a healthy recreation component. Underbrink-Curran saw the Alliance as an aid in improving relations between recreational and agricultural users, an arena where conflict frequently occurred. She also noted that the Alliance involved county governments. And when people saw their local government involved, which they trust to watch out for their concerns, everyone won — the federal land managers, local residents, and visitors.

By their actions, residents of the Colorado drainage have demonstrated that a vital water resource contributes to community pride and quality of life. In doing so, these citizens have inadvertently applied what in some circles might be considered the radical concept of "bioregionalism"— communities integrated with their local ecosystems. The "bio" in bioregionalism calls for a human society more closely related to nature, and the "region" refers to a greater consciousness of place. For too long, many along the Front Range have viewed the Colorado River basin as little more than a resource providing the raw material — water — so critical to economic engines. Only time will tell if the bioregional efforts of local communities succeed in redefining the Colorado River as a place faithful to its nature.

*Horses graze along Rock Creek, a tributary of the Colorado River, Eagle County*

Riparian habitats fill an important niche in Rocky Mountain ecosystems. The banks of rivers and streams bring together a diverse array of flora and fauna, leading biologists to consider riparian zones the most productive of all ecological communities. Streams also frequently serve as early warning indicators of ecological disruption. For example, macroinvertebrates, the creatures that inhabit the undersides of river rocks, are highly sensitive to changes in aquatic chemistry. By monitoring changes in their abundance and type, scientists can assess the impact of upstream development on water quality. Riparian corridors serve another role, for they form critical links across the landscape. Streams connect various ecological zones and provide travel corridors for species both large and small. The budding science of conservation biology concerns itself with maintaining the natural diversity of ecosystems and retaining vital arteries between them.

*Springtime along Brush Creek, a tributary of the Eagle River, White River National Forest*

*Storm runoff on Hayes Creek Falls, a tributary of the Crystal River, White River National Forest*
*Overleaf: A clearing storm over the headwaters of Cataract Creek, a tributary of the Blue River,*
*Eagles Nest Wilderness*

*Snowmass Mountain, elevation 14,092 feet, the source of Snowmass Creek — a tributary of the Roaring Fork River, Maroon Bells-Snowmass Wilderness*

The Colorado River offers one of the last sanctuaries for several native fish species — the Colorado River squawfish, the humpback chub, the bonytail chub, and the razorback sucker. All of these fish evolved in the natural flow of the Colorado, a regimen that included raging spring floods of muddy, ice-cold snowmelt and languid, warm, low water in late summer. The fish developed uncommon survival mechanisms to thrive in this wildly fluctuating environment. Water diversion, inundation, and extensive water flow and temperature modifications from large dams decimated the fish, and today they survive only in the Colorado River below Grand Junction, in the Yampa River in Dinosaur National Monument, and in one or two other locations. Ruby Canyon, on the Colorado near the Utah state line, boasts one of the healthiest surviving squawfish populations and is designated critical habitat for both the squawfish and other endangered fish.

*The Colorado River in Ruby Canyon, Black Ridge Canyons BLM Wilderness Study Area*

Streamflows drop to their lowest levels in late fall and winter. For trout and other aquatic life, these are critical periods because available habitat shrinks to a minimum. Traditionally, there have been few demands for extensive water diversions in winter, for irrigation of agricultural fields and the watering of urban landscapes are nonexistent at this time of year. Today, however, ski resorts place increasing demands on winter streamflows for water to make artificial snow. Snow-making extends the ski season by allowing resorts to open earlier, and it also guarantees against economically disastrous snow droughts. The environmental downside to this practice comes with the increased stress that winter diversions place on streams. The conflicting claims on water for snow-making and for maintaining minimum winter streamflows create one more challenging balancing act for Colorado water planners.

*Autumn colors along Avalanche Creek, a tributary of the Crystal River, White River National Forest*

*The Eagle River in winter, Eagle County*

*The Fryingpan River, a tributary of the Roaring Fork River, White River National Forest*

Biologists with the Colorado Division of Wildlife designate streams with exceptionally high-quality aquatic habitat as Gold Medal fisheries. These streams contain a high percentage of trout greater than fourteen inches in length, and the management emphasis is on providing trophy trout fishing opportunities and angler success. Fishing on all such streams is limited to artificial flies and lures, and in some instances, such as on the Fryingpan River, it is restricted to catch-and-release in order to increase fish populations and sizes. Nine Colorado streams are designated Gold Medal waters, and foremost among these is the stretch of the Fryingpan River below Ruedi Reservoir near the town of Basalt. On any given day on the Fryingpan, a skilled few of Colorado's 400,000 resident fishermen might be observed matching wits with the river's wily trout.

*Churning rapids challenge the best of whitewater enthusiasts in Gore Canyon,
Colorado River, near Kremmling*

It is hard to imagine that the Colorado River both begins and ends as a trickle. The hardest working of all western rivers, the Colorado has so many human demands placed upon it that its entire annual flow of 15 million acre-feet is consumed before the river ever reaches the Gulf of Mexico. The pitiful remnants of the mighty Colorado sink into the shifting sands of its riverbed south of the Morelos Dam in Mexico. One cannot ignore the Colorado's fate, even while contemplating its birth high in Rocky Mountain National Park. Here, before the river barely gets going, Colorado's Front Range grabs the first of the 500,000 acre-feet of water annually diverted across the Continental Divide. One early diversion was the 14-mile Grand Ditch, constructed in 1900. The Grand Ditch collects water from a dozen tributaries in the Never Summer Range and diverts it across the Divide at an elevation of 10,200 feet.

*Early autumn along the Blue River, Arapaho National Forest*

*The beginnings of the mighty Colorado River, Rocky Mountain National Park*

# THE YAMPA

## PARTNERSHIPS FOR PRESERVATION

Many call the Yampa Colorado's last free-flowing river, but this isn't quite true; the Yampa is neither the last nor is it entirely free flowing. In this case, river proponents use "free flowing" as a metaphor for natural river behavior, for the Yampa still responds to its primeval patterns of spring flood, channel meandering, siltation, and fall drought. Other Colorado rivers, like the San Miguel near Telluride (a focus of preservation efforts by The Nature Conservancy) and the Crystal River near Redstone, also flow freely and with relatively little evidence of human alteration. Unlike the Yampa, these are short mountain rivers generally confined to narrow valleys. In contrast, the Yampa drains large areas of rolling rangeland on its 240-mile course through northwestern Colorado. This corner of the state is sparsely populated, high, and cold, and consequently it is less suited for intensive agricultural developments than areas along the Front Range or in the Grand Valley near Grand Junction. Lack of development pressures has, fortunately, left the Yampa largely undiminished.

Despite its appellation as free flowing, the Yampa is not entirely free of dams. A half-dozen or more impoundments lie scattered throughout its headwaters, including two main-stem dams above Steamboat Springs. But by and large, enough tributaries still run unchecked to let the river follow its ancient patterns. The combination of a large drainage basin and natural ecological processes makes the Yampa unique in Colorado, and perhaps throughout the entire Colorado River basin. The river's singularly pristine ecological condition gives Coloradans a clean canvas on which to paint a cooperative vision of human and natural coexistence.

To understand the remarkable adaptations necessary for life to flourish in a widely gyrating environment such as the Yampa's, it first helps to consider the environmental conditions. The Yampa's headwaters include Buffalo Pass in the Park Range east of Steamboat Springs. This pass receives more snowfall, 300 inches per year, than any other location in Colorado. In spring, lengthening days and increased solar radiation melt the snowpack, saturating the soil until the melted snow flows into innumerable creeks and streams that eventually merge into the major tributaries of the Yampa. The rushing water overflows low floodplains until the Yampa is a roiling, unruly, ice-cold torrent. When spring runoff subsides, the once-impassable river turns into a tepid, mild-mannered channel only ankle deep in many places.

Given these environmental extremes, the evolution of a notable variety of life forms, which have necessarily developed extraordinary adaptive mechanisms, comes as little surprise. Biodiversity is the catchall scientific phrase for diversity of life on earth, and the Yampa contributes more than its fair share to global biodiversity for a number of reasons — the river retains an extensive riparian deciduous forest, and it plays host to the last stronghold of four native, but now endangered, species of fish.

One need not be a university-educated forester to appreciate the grace and beauty of the Yampa's verdant cottonwood forests. Travelers along Highway 40 between Steamboat Springs and Craig cannot help but notice this belt of greenery. And as is so often the case in nature, an intricate and delicate connection exists between ecological processes, such as the Yampa's vacillating hydrology and the thriving population of migratory birds attracted to the river's forest.

Scientists who study river dynamics call the Yampa's meanderings the "dance of the river." A predictable pattern underlies the Yampa's apparently random fluctuations. At high water velocities, the river carries great loads of sediment. Where the water slows, such as at the inside bend of a curve, the river drops sediment and the floodplain grows. At the outside of a bend, where the water's velocity is greatest, the river's current undercuts banks and eats away the existing floodplain. During floods, the bends sharpen and the river changes course to find the path of least resistance. Some of the extreme bends are left behind, turning into shallow backwaters called oxbows. In this fashion, the river slowly dances back and forth, continually creating new channels and destroying old floodplains.

Coincidental with the river's dance, spring snowmelt overflows its banks into the floodplain and scours the gravel beds just prior to the dropping of seeds by narrowleaf cottonwoods. This process creates fertile conditions for regeneration of the riparian forests, resulting in cottonwoods and willows that range from seedlings to stately giants. These multi-aged forests sustain migratory birds in abundance, for different birds occupy different layers of the forest canopy. If some age classes of trees are lost through misdirected management, some species of migratory birds may disappear.

These complex ecological relationships pose new challenges for The Nature Conservancy's efforts to preserve biodiversity. Conservancy scientists recognize that a

---

*Above the Grand Overhang, on the Yampa River, Dinosaur National Monument*

strategy of preserving isolated stands of riparian forests is inadequate if the underlying ecological processes that create them are not similarly preserved. In response, the Conservancy initiated an Upper Colorado River Basin Bioreserve program to integrate natural processes, such as river hydrology, with biological inventories of rare plant assemblages. The Yampa offers the first practical application of this approach in Colorado.

Mark Burget, the Conservancy's bioreserve director, explains that this program intends to apply ecosystem concepts on a grand scale instead of just focusing on specific sites. By preserving large-scale ecological processes such as river flood cycles, Conservancy scientists can perpetuate the Yampa's riparian forests, migratory birds, and native fishes. The last of these, the Yampa's native endangered fish species, may be the greatest beneficiary of the bioreserve concept.

Four native fish species inhabit the Yampa — Colorado squawfish, humpback chub, bonytail chub, and razorback sucker. Though they lack glamorous names, these fish are ecological survivors of the first order. Consider their native environment — a river that fluctuates between ice-cold, silt-choked spring floods and clear, lukewarm, late summer flows. Not surprisingly, these native species evolved unique adaptations that permit them to thrive under inhospitable conditions. Unfortunately for the fish, extensive water diversions that deplete spring flows and dams that depress late summer water temperatures alter the ecological balance on many western rivers. This newly created environment and altered hydrologic cycles have disrupted thousands of years of evolutionary adaptation.

The Colorado squawfish has long been ridiculed as a trash fish, and, in fact, wildlife managers in the 1960s actively poisoned rivers to eliminate squawfish and other native species. The squawfish, however, deserves a better reputation. It evolved as the main predator in the Yampa, and as such it occupies an aquatic ecological role similar to that of wolves and grizzlies on land. Though a member of the minnow family, the Colorado squawfish is the largest member native to North America, historically growing to more than six feet in length and weighing more than 100 pounds, with a life-span of 25 to 50 years. Like the riparian forests and their associated bird life, squawfish adapted to the Yampa's variable environment. They evolved a spawning response that is initiated only when water temperatures exceed 68 degrees Fahrenheit, which corresponds to low, late summer flows that leave slack pools in side channels. Squawfish young thrive in these warm, shallow backwaters. High spring flows are also needed to scour the side channels, sweeping substrate pebbles free of fine silt prior to spawning. Water depletions that reduce spring floods, and dams that restrict migration and alter water temperatures substantially, inhibit the evolutionary advantages acquired over eons by the squawfish.

Burget emphasizes the dependence of the fish on river cycles. "The only way to preserve the fish is by maintaining some form of the natural environment," he says. But he also knows that the Yampa has more than a century of human settlement and development. "The challenge of the bioreserve program is to integrate human uses of land and water with our mission of biological diversity. That means working with local communities in a way that serves them and yet also preserves the biological diversity of the area."

The Nature Conservancy opened a field office in the upper Yampa Valley to maintain a visible and accessible presence. "We can't achieve conservation on the local level without an office that is responsive to community members," says Burget. The Conservancy wants to create a win-win situation where private landowners are motivated through economic incentives to manage their lands for conservation purposes, thereby simultaneously preserving biological diversity. In this respect, the Conservancy is applying lessons learned through its successful involvement in overseas conservation efforts. In Latin America, for example, the Conservancy recognized the impossibility of imposing an outside vision on local cultures and lifestyles. There are a number of parallels to this in the United States, for many of this country's biologically diverse habitats are on private lands. By involving local communities, listening to their concerns, and devising strategies that recognize the needs of all parties, the Conservancy hopes that its pioneering Yampa River bioreserve project will show that preserving biological diversity is to everyone's advantage.

*The Green River as it winds through Browns Park National Wildlife Refuge*

Some call Colorado the "Mother of Rivers" or the "Headwaters State" because it is the source of many of the West's major rivers. The exception is the Green River, which flows into the state of Colorado. The Green begins high in the Wind River Mountains in western Wyoming. As the river heads south, Utah's Uinta Mountains deflect it eastward, where it winds through Colorado's northwest corner. During its short journey through Colorado, the Green River cuts through two distinctive landforms — wide, pastoral Browns Park and the narrow Canyon of Lodore in Dinosaur National Monument. The Green drains a greater watershed than the Colorado River, and by the time it finally combines with the Colorado in Canyonlands National Park in central Utah, it is the larger of the two.

*Evening light along the Green River, Browns Park National Wildlife Refuge*

*Passing storm, East Fork Williams Fork of the Yampa River, Routt County*
*Overleaf: Sunset on the Green River, Browns Park National Wildlife Refuge*

As part of his epic exploration of the Colorado River system in 1869, John Wesley Powell successfully navigated the Canyon of Lodore, located in what is now Dinosaur National Monument. Although Powell and his party gained their rapid-running baptism in a series of small rapids upstream in Flaming Gorge, the Canyon of Lodore offered the first real test of that skill. Powell referred to the rapids as "falls" in deference to their powerful hydraulic action. The first catastrophe of his expedition occurred several miles below the Gates of Lodore where one boat unintentionally ran a particularly severe rapid and was smashed against the rocks. Because he incorrectly supposed that Ashley's 1825 expedition met the same fate on this rapid, Powell named it "Disaster Falls." Powell's men had better luck several days later when they portaged their gear around another turbulent, boulder-strewn stretch of river which Powell christened "Hell's Half-Mile."

*The Gates of Lodore, where the Green River enters Dinosaur National Monument*

*North Fork of the White River, a tributary of the Green River, White River National Forest*

*The Little Snake River, a tributary of the Yampa River, originates in the Mount Zirkel Wilderness*

In recent years Colorado's conservation community has expanded its means for safeguarding threatened river segments to include the acquisition of minimum streamflows. The Yampa River offers the last best opportunity in Colorado to preserve a river that follows natural rhythms. Many of the Yampa's native life forms, including riparian deciduous forests, their associated migratory bird life, and four endangered fish species, depend on one unaltered ecological process of the river — its substantial spring floods. The floods provide fertile ground for renewal of the willow and cottonwood forests and are crucial to successful spawning for the endangered fish. One option under consideration to secure the needed streamflow entails the purchase of water rights held by the Colorado River Water Conservation District, which once planned to dam the main stem of the Yampa.

*West of the town of Craig, a ten-mile stretch of the Yampa River penetrates a pristine roadless area managed by the Bureau of Land Management*

Steamboat Rock stands as a silent sentinel above the confluence of the Green and Yampa rivers at Echo Park in Dinosaur National Monument. Echo Park was not always so quiet, however.  Modern America's greatest conflict between preservation and water resource development occurred here in the 1950s. As part of its gargantuan plan to harness the Colorado River and all its tributaries, the U.S. Bureau of Reclamation proposed construction of a dam at Echo Park, which would have created a giant reservoir flooding both the Green and Yampa rivers. American conservationists, led by the Sierra Club's David Brower, drew a line in the sand and firmly rejected this desecration of a national park system unit. Brower prevailed, and today Steamboat Rock oversees a vibrant, living river rather than the stagnant waters of yet another lifeless reservoir. Unfortunately, the dam builders at the Bureau of Reclamation aimed their sights elsewhere, and the Colorado River's pristine Glen Canyon has been forever submerged under Lake Powell.

*The Elk River emanates from the Mount Zirkel Wilderness and empties into the Yampa River near Steamboat Springs*

*Steamboat Rock towers above the Yampa River, Dinosaur National Monument*

*Cross Mountain Gorge and the Yampa River, Cross Mountain BLM Wilderness Study Area*